Mark Fi
Fitness Business Secrets

Lessons, Stories, and True Life Shenanigans from the World's Only Multi-Million Dollar Glittery Unicorn Fitness Cult

Mark Fisher

Copyright © 2023 Mark Fisher

All rights reserved.

ISBN: 979-8-218-08682-4

CONTENTS

An Introduction

The first thing to know is that *this book is about you.*

It's about your hopes, your fears, and your dreams.

If you're reading this book, my bet is you're a current or aspiring gym owner looking to help more people, grow your income, and leverage your expertise as a fitness professional to create a business you love.

This means you have chosen a professional path that is 1) worthwhile and 2) difficult.

I know this because I have chosen the same path as you.

Although this book is about you, I'd like to share a bit about my background. This will help you understand a bit more about your friendly author and the background that informs my philosophies on running a training gym.

In 2011, after years of working as a one-on-one independent personal trainer in NYC, I decided to focus my efforts and see if I could make it into a "real business."

You see, I had spent years developing my craft as a fitness professional. But now I wanted to build something more substantial; something that could impact more people and build a more sustainable and creatively satisfying lifestyle.

The previous summer I had started cycling business books into my usual professional reading. I launched a six-week makeover program that developed a cult following in the Broadway community. Shortly after seeing some traction, I decided to burn the boats. My best friend from high school, Michael Keeler, came onboard as my business partner. We made a few hires and we got a lease.

Mark Fisher Fitness was no longer just a one man band. Mark

Fisher Fitness, the brick and mortar training gym, was born.

In spite of being in one of the most competitive markets in the country, we were full of hope and excitement about our potential.

For those not familiar with MFF, it's fair to say we're a pretty unusual place. Our tagline is "Ridiculous Humans, Serious Fitness." And for over 10 years, we have *lived* this mantra. We've sought to marry best-in-class training, nutrition, and behavior change coaching and cover it in a chocolate sauce of madness.

On the one hand, it was an organic choice to leverage my natural eccentricities. I loved to teach fitness concepts using humor, potty language, and fantastical and subversive imagery and metaphors. But beyond knowing *myself*, I knew *my people* — the ones who didn't feel spoken to by most of the fitness industry — and I bet they would be drawn to our soaring freakflag.

Instead of calling our members "clients," we call them Ninjas. Instead of referring to our home as a "gym," we named it The Enchanted Ninja Clubhouse of Glory and Dreams. The space itself is colorful and glittery; our design aesthetic can best be described as "5-year-old on LSD." Our spiritual mascot is the humble and majestic unicorn. And from our birth, our mission has been to create a place where the other kids who ate lunch alone in middle school would feel welcomed, even if gym class wasn't our favorite subject.

We've had a damn good run. 50% of all small businesses fail in the first five years, and only 33% make it to year ten. At the time of this writing, we're in our eleventh year and going strong.

We've had some amazing results in that time. We've worked with over 6,000 Ninjas. We've had over 100 MFFers (team members). And we've done over $30 million in revenue. We ranked as the 312th fastest growing business in America in 2015's Inc 500. We've also been named one of Men's Health's Top Gyms in America. We've been covered by local and national press both inside the fitness industry and in mainstream publications like *The New York Times, Forbes, the Wall St Journal, Details*, and many, many more.

As more and more fitness professionals caught wind of the looney unicorn gym, we started fielding consulting requests. Keeler and I soon started a second company called **Business for Unicorns** to share what we were learning. Over the past few years, we've spent hundreds and hundreds of hours doing one-on-one coaching and delivering talks and workshops to thousands of gym owners.

Thanks to BFU, I've had the opportunity to travel the world giving keynotes, lectures, and workshops at Perform Better, IDEA World, IDEA Club & Studio, IDEA Personal Trainer Institute, FILEX, SCW MANIA, Anytime Fitness Australia, The Summit by BFS, Lift the Bar, The Fitness Business Summit, The International Fitness Business Alliance, The Strong Pro Summit, Vigor Ground Summit, Mike Boyle Strength and Conditioning, Strength Matters, Kansas City Fitness Summit, Nor-Cal Summit, Fitness Revolution, VASA Fitness, UK Leisure Industry Week, and many more.

Outside of fitness, I've been a speaker, mentor, and/or consultant for businesses and events outside the fitness industry, including SONY Music, Security Scorecard, Two12, Red Door by Elizabeth Arden, Novus Surgical, LiquiTech, TEDxBroadway, and more.

Recently, I even launched a third company as an investor to open up multiple locations of Alloy Personal Training, an emerging franchise brand.

I hope this doesn't sound like bragging. Believe me when I say the above feathers in my cap are NOT the reasons why I think you should listen to me.

You should listen to me because I have been in the trenches, just like you, operating a training gym.

I've opened — and closed — a second location of Mark Fisher Fitness in New York City. (The full story is in this book.)

I've struggled with suddenly being tight on cash and not understanding how it was possible to be profitable but low on cash flow.

Just like you, I've been wracked with anxiety that I didn't know what the hell I was doing when:

Negotiating leases with landlords…

Fighting off stress-induced canker sores the first time I had to let an employee go…

Blundering my way through endlessly changing digital marketing strategies…

Figuring out how to onboard new team members without leaving them in tears…

Getting whacked with a massive and unexpected multiple five-figure bill…

Being completely screwed out of hundreds of thousands of dollars by an inept team of contractors…

Or any other number of situations that left me feeling like crawling back into my bed.

Over the past 10 years, I've had more painful conversations than I can count. I've heard many things that were tough to hear. And I've shared many things that were tough to say.

Just like you, I've struggled with conflict between myself and my team when I was too insecure to set boundaries.

When I was too afraid to do what I knew was in the business's best interest.

When I let friendship get in the way of making the right call.

When I was called out by my team for something that was totally unfair and based on misperceptions and ugly assumptions.

When I was called out by my team for something that was completely on me and reflective of an embarrassing leadership failing.

When I messed something up and could tell some trust in my competence had been lost.

I've had to navigate the never-ending tension between wanting to support my team's personal aspirations with the requirement to protect MFF and the team as a whole.

Just like you, I've gotten highly personal criticisms from long time clients I considered friends; sometimes fair, sometimes not so much.

I've experienced the pain of clients feeling let down or frustrated by a change of service, a price increase, or a team member dropping a major ball in our client experience.

I've received cutting and confusing feedback delivered anonymously with no way for me to ask clarifying questions.

I've struggled to keep the peace on more than one occasion when a volatile and contentious issue was tearing our community apart with clients on both sides demanding MFF take their preferred action.

And of course, though it barely needs to be said, I've also faced the financial and emotional headwinds of a worldwide pandemic; having to let go of our entire team, launching an online business overnight, and scratching and clawing our way back one client at a time.

A pandemic that, at the time of this writing, is not yet done and is still materially impacting NYC as a market for in-person fitness services.

Now…

I realize the above sounds heavy. Sorry if it caused any PTSD!

I want to be very clear. I LOVE my job. I love it. I LOVE what I get to do, I love our clients, and I love my team.

I'm not sharing the above to imply that I don't love what I do.

I'm sharing it to say I know the unique joys and challenges of the work that we do.

I'm not some full time consultant. I can understand why someone would go that way. It's a hell of a lot less work! And maybe that will be my path one day. After all, we should all stay open to what possibilities the future may have in store.

But today?

Today I am a gym owner.

So I know your training business is your life's work. It's how you hope to improve society, positively impact the world, and create a livelihood to support your family.

Because of the success — and batshit shenanigans — of Mark Fisher Fitness, it could be easy to discount us as wild outliers with little to teach.

But you and I are not so different. Not in the ways that matter most.

And what I most want you to know, whether you've had your gym for 25 years or are scheming and dreaming about opening up your very own spot…

You are not alone.

I'm right alongside you. Marching onward, growing, learning, loving and doing the damn work.

Thank you so much for taking the time to read this book. I put my whole heart into it. I know it can help you achieve your goals more quickly, all while hopefully sidestepping some of my errors.

Jumping high five with my entire f*cking soul,

Mark

May 20th, 2022

****

The book you're about to read is a compilation of blog posts written for BusinessForUnicorns.com.

Throughout this book, I'll occasionally make references to additional resources. You can download them for free at businessforunicorns.com/book-stuff.

And if you like my musings, here are three other (free) resources to get more MF and Business for Unicorns magic...

MarkFisherYouTube.com - This is my YouTube channel. It's my very favorite thing I get to do. If you like reading my words, you may like hearing me say words while watching my face move (*a lot*). You will learn stuff and hopefully get some LOLs.

GymOwnerReportCard.com - Do you ever feel a bit overwhelmed about *all* the things you need to do in order to run your training gym? That makes sense! This is a really cool tool that will help you identify how you're doing in each of the core functions of running your training gym.

BusinessForUnicorns.com/Podcast - This is our podcast. You'll get to hear myself, Michael Keeler, Pete Dupuis, Ben Pickard, and a whole array of fitness business smartypants peeps. Subscribe to us on your preferred podcast app and we shall beam fitness knowledge directly into your earholes.

Also, you can follow me on **@markfisherhumanbeing** on Instagram. I don't post too much, but you can always send me a DM to say hi and/or show me pictures of puppies and stuff.

10 Ways to Grow Your Training Gym

Time sensitive offers are a great way to encourage your prospects to finally try out — or return to — your training gym.

Now there's a bit of an art to this. We don't want to "train" our audience to always wait for something special. But a clear call to action and a compelling reason to *take action now* is a powerful tool.

To that end, below are 10 ideas for time sensitive offers. Some are for never-been-members, others are for former members, and some are for unconverted trial participants.

As a reminder, for this to work, **there needs to be a deadline**. ("If they can do it *whenever*, they'll do it *never."*) It can be a date when the offer ends, a limited number of spots, or both. All of the below options presume you're using one or both of these strategies.

While I've included some discounted offers below, remember, this will always hurt your profitability and lifetime customer value. So when possible, focus on value adds, OR one-time discounts that don't lock in lowered rates. Cash discounts can serve a place. But use them sparingly, and make sure you understand how this impacts your cashflow.

NOTE: You'll need to decide how to apply this to your business. Some offers work better for small group personal training, and others work better for class models. But even if a given offer doesn't make sense for you, try to unpack how it could be modified to work for your biz.

10 Ways to Grow Your Training Gym

1. One free (usually paid) trial for clients to give away to one friend
2. Limited time offer to sign up for a (usually paid) trial for only $1
3. Sign up for any new membership and get a value add (extra

pack of sessions, nutrition consult, free month for a friend, free swag, etc.)

4. Sign up for any new membership and get $50 or $100 off your 1st month
5. Limited time offer to buy packs of sessions (if you only offer monthly memberships)
6. A temporary one-month complimentary upgrade for a select number of current members
7. Claim a free month as a "We want you back" offer for a select number of former members
8. Sign up for a year-long paid-in-full membership and get a 13th month free
9. Sign up for a new membership with a friend and each person gets a value add or discount on 1st month
10. Limited time offer for unconverted trial prospects to get access to your current intro offer

Looking for even *more* strategies? Head to businessforunicorns.com/book-stuff for more.

How Do I Find Good Employees for My Training Gym? [15 Ways]

Finding qualified team members is one of the biggest challenges of owning a training gym. And the stakes are high to get it right.

Small organizations are *massively* impacted by each new hire: their energy levels, their values, their skill sets, their emotional intelligence, etc. After all, when you run a service business, you're largely selling the life force of the humans your clients interact with. Furthermore, each team member can either bring up — or bring down — the rest of your team.

At the time of this writing, it's a particularly tough environment to find new team members. Many businesses are struggling to find people. While there are all sorts of theories as to why, it's pretty consistent across industries.

This means there are actually training gyms at or near capacity because they *can't find enough staff to service the demand.* Yikes!

Here a smattering of thoughts and tips for finding good employees.

1) Accept It Will Be 10x Harder Than You Think It Should Be

After eleven plus years as an operator — and years of coaching other training gym owners — this is the biggest mental block I see.

Not unlike marketing for clients, many training gym owners can't get their heads around how much time, energy, and effort needs to go into the hiring process.

You can't put up a "We're hiring!" page on your website and fill the role next week. Expect to spend 10x more time, energy, and effort than intuitively feels reasonable.

You need to turn over every possible rock to look for candidates:

- Make a personal outreach to individuals in your network that could be a fit or may know leads
- Share your job description with your clients via individual emails, group email, or private FB group posts; offer them a referral bonus for bringing you leads
- Post on every possible job board (Indeed, ZipRecruiter, etc.)
- Consider paying to boost these posts
- Consider hiring a fitness industry-specific recruiter
- Identify current or former clients who fit your values and could be trained up for the role you're looking for
- Network with local colleges
- Build an internship program
- Leverage public social media posts
- Ask your team for intros to leads; consider offering them a referral bonus
- Attend continuing education events and network with potential candidates
- Have a prominently highlighted hiring section on your website
- Work out at local gyms and studios and look for talent
- Look at the Instagrams of local gyms and studios to look for talent
- Start a relationship with employees who provide you a great customer service experience, even if it's in another industry

… you have to do EVERYTHING to get the word out.

Just like generating leads for your training gym, this is a numbers game.

2) Build Your Pipeline *Before You Need It*

The very best way to do this is with an internship program.

Based on your market and training gym — and the role you're hiring — this won't always be viable. But if you *can,* it's illuminating to work with individuals for a few months before making hiring decisions. You'll have a WAY better idea who will actually be a good fit for your organization.

Beyond having an internship, it's also a good idea to start and build relationships with potential future employees before you need to make a hire. This is obviously most important for trainers, as you need a specific set of skills. But the same can be said for administrative staff.

Most of the skills in a training gym can be learned via training; even trainer roles, given sufficient time. So always keep your eye out for talent. Proactively snag contact info for the amazing waiter or barista and develop a relationship with them.

And of course, for many training gyms, your clientele base will be a great source of potential new hires. Not only do they already know your culture, but you can find out a lot about someone via your experience with them as a client.

3) Make Your Hiring Process Your Most Dialed In SOP

Most training gyms simply don't have to hire all that often. And when you don't have much experience doing something and can't get in many reps… you tend to suck. This is why you must create a clearly documented system that you run — and improve! — each and every time you make a hire.

You will get better over time at hiring. But you have to be intentional about documenting your process and results. Since you won't be doing a bunch of hires month after month, having a set of SOPs and careful notes are necessary to see improvement over time.

For instance, we've learned the hard way at MFF that we need to put our candidates in uncomfortable and stressful situations ("a stress test") to see how they handle pressure. We've seen how results vary if we skip this step.

Your SOP should include things like scripts, interview questions, target number of candidates for each step of the funnel, and the order in which you execute each of the above-mentioned funnels.

4) Accept You Won't Get It Right Some of the Time

While having an internship will be the very best way to improve your odds, making hires isn't an exact science; especially without an extended internship dating period. You're going to make a wrong hire from time to time.

On the one hand, you have a responsibility to the individual — and your own sanity — to create an amazing onboarding experience that sets people up for success. Commit to upskilling how you onboard new employees. Don't let a poor onboarding and training process thwart a new employee's potential.

But on the other hand, you have to be willing to fire fast. When it becomes clear someone isn't working out, you've got to make the tough call. This is a bitter pill to swallow when you realize just how time intensive it is to hire and onboard someone (see the first point). Furthermore, it has a real cost to make staffing changes when you only have a small crew. And of course, it's pretty much the WORST part of owning a business.

But it bears repeating: in a small organization each team member has an outsize impact on the results of the business. Holding on to someone who's not able to perform does no one any favors; including the individual that could probably find a better fit elsewhere.

NOTE: One of the most common missteps in all of business is holding on to an underperforming employee for too long.

The 5 Pillars of Marketing

Training gym owners often find one marketing channel and rely on it completely. This leaves you vulnerable if something disrupts said channel.

(iOS updates to Facebook tracking, anyone?)

When I'm helping a client grow their training gym, we use a simple framework to make sure they're fishing with multiple "poles in the water."

It's imperative that you create multiple strategies to build awareness around your business, so prospective clients get to know you, like you, and trust you.

Prospects don't buy when YOU're ready, they buy when THEY're ready. So you need to build that trust in advance. And then when the time DOES come, you're the person they hire.

So how do we do this?

Through the 5 Pillars of Training Gym Marketing.

1) Email Marketing

If you don't have a curated list of emails of people who already know you, and presumably like and trust you, start here.

Spend a few hours with your phone and email contact list and create your list.

Email your list *at least 1x per week* with value-building content that does three things: educates, inspires, and/or entertains. This is best done by sharing solutions to the problems your prospects are having.

Always include a clear CTA for what to do next when they're ready to work with you. Just don't hard-sell all the time, focus on giving value first.

2) Organic Social Media

Organic social media is another channel for people to know, like, and trust you.

Social media strategy is similar in principle to email; it's a channel to educate, entertain, and inspire. Different platforms have different best practices for making your content pop. But the key thing is doing *something* on the regular.

At the time of this writing, the most popular platform to get organic traction for most training gyms is Instagram.

In a perfect world, create 3x-7x feed posts per week, and 1x-5x stories per day.

Warning: there's a point of diminishing returns where time spent doesn't have a positive ROI on your business. Remember, you're there (primarily) to create and GIVE, not to consume!

3) Offline Marketing

This is the most common missing bucket for training gym owners. Which is too bad. Because it can be easier to break through since no one else is doing it.

This broad category includes all the ways you can grow your business *without* digital marketing. Examples include Direct Mail, newspaper ads, billboards, partnerships with local businesses, sponsorships of local sports teams, events for local charities, etc.

Different strategies will be more or less helpful depending on your market. And admittedly, offline channels are a bit harder to track. But this isn't impossible to solve. Just be sure to 1) create a unique URL for the landing pages where you direct prospects and 2) be sure to ask all new prospects how they heard about you.

Remember, marketing is a synonym for "test."

4) Referral Marketing

If you're great at what you do, you likely already get a fair amount of organic referrals. While this is great, you want to create systems to incentivize and explicitly ask your clients for intros to friends.

When we think about referral marketing, we can consider two buckets:

- Evergreen Referral Promos - Ongoing strategies that offer incentives in cash, service, or status in exchange for intros that result in leads, trials, or new members

- Dedicated Referral Pushes - Specific periods of time where you put effort and energy into highlighting existing referral incentives AND/OR add *extra* bonuses/contests for activities that intro leads, trials, or new members to your business.

5) Paid Digital Marketing

Paid digital marketing costs have gone up a LOT over the last few years. This is especially true for Facebook/Instagram. However, paid digital can still play a key role in gathering leads for your training gym.

Just realize that 1) it can't be your only pillar and 2) the leads will tend to be colder and less qualified. So for this to be fruitful, you need a strong system to nurture the leads.

Remember, all these strategies work together. Paid digital marketing can serve a place in building brand awareness so people know you. But ideally some/most of your efforts are focused on making compelling offers that capture contact info so you can keep the relationship going.

The most common compelling offers are:

- "Lead magnets" (free report, recipe guide, video series, etc.)
- Free workout(s)

- Free week
- Strategy sessions
- Low barrier offers

And when you get their contact info?

Short Term Magic: Follow up to encourage them to use what they signed up for. Sometimes this will work, and sometimes it won't. When it doesn't…

Long Term Magic: Ongoing email and social media marketing so they come to like you and trust you over time.

3 Considerations [Managing Change]

Here's a simple framework for managing change.

Let's say you've been thinking on a critical issue for a while. You've invited feedback from other people to improve your thinking, and you've come to the conclusion that it's time to make a hard decision. The next step is to break the news. And how you break the news will have a big impact on how it's received.

One of the arts of business is balancing decisive action and speed against a consideration of the second and third order consequences. Particularly if the changes are not to every stakeholder's liking.

Here are three quick thoughts to keep in mind anytime you're planning to "rip off a band-aid."

1) Dial in the Communication

This could be an email announcement to clients, a meeting held for your team, or a one-on-one phone call. While the channel will vary, it's important to think through how best to deliver the news.

This means providing as much clarity as possible on:

- Why - Clearly and transparently laying out the reasons for change.
- What - Communicate what exactly is being changed as clearly as possible.
- Who - Identify who is being impacted and how, as well as Where and When.
- What Else - Anticipate concerns and follow-up questions.

If at all possible, you don't want to rush this prep. If it's a big change, you may need to do three or four drafts of your email or presentation. If it's a one-on-one chat, you may need to roleplay. And you'll almost certainly benefit from getting outside feedback to identify your blindspots.

2) Expect Emotions and Make That Ok

It's also important to think through the emotional impact of any change. As one of my mentors Ari Weinzweig says, the first step to organizational change is resistance.

This is normal. Even when it's truly an immediate positive impact for all parties, most people will still have some discomfort with change.

And frankly, change that is in the aggregate best interest often has negative impacts on some stakeholders. If you've really taken the time to sit with an issue and it's clear making a given change is the best move, you should still do it. But follow the guidelines from Step 1 and be sensitive and thoughtful about how people may feel.

It's ok for people to be upset. You shouldn't be surprised or annoyed with them for not immediately getting onboard with your vision. Remember, change is tough. Be patient and receptive to their concerns while making it clear what parts of a given decision are no longer up for debate.

3) "Don't Piss On My Face and Tell Me It's Raining"

One of the worst things you can do is try to spin a change as an "exciting opportunity!" when it's going to clearly make some things worse for some individuals.

This is the kind of corporate shit we ALL hate. Resist the desire to hide behind spin.

To be clear, I'm not encouraging you to be overly apologetic. After all, you're making a necessary change that's in the aggregate best interest of all stakeholders. You can and should emphasize the benefits of a given change. But it's ok to acknowledge the places where people may not be pleased and sincerely empathize.

****

All of this is predicated on making a difficult decision that is truly in everyone's overall best interest. The job of the leader is to do their good faith best to balance the competing interests of all stakeholders to arrive at the best overall solution. And remember, this can't happen without inviting thought partners who will help you see blindspots. So as a rule, these kinds of decisions shouldn't be made in a vacuum, as none of us are infallible.

But once you've "baked out the potato," have the courage of your convictions to make the call. And be thoughtful in how you roll it out.

How to Get — and Stay — Focused

At the highest level, time management has two master buckets.

1. Making the Plan
2. Executing the Plan

The first bit requires a consideration of your goals and values against all the ways you could spend your time. You have to prioritize what should happen when and in what order. Then you need to schedule your projects and tasks to be done at certain times.

But that's only the first part.

If you're a wiz at making the perfect plan but always get derailed, it doesn't matter how good you are at planning.

To actually succeed... *you have to do the damn thing.*

And yet, for many of us, staying focused is quite a challenge.

It can be helpful to identify — and solve for — three distinct kinds of interruptions.

1) Physical Interruptions - This is when your team or clients or family members physically ask for your intention while you're attempting deep work on a task.

This one is relatively simple to solve (with the exception of very small humans). Just communicate your needs, or if needed/ possible, find a private place to work.

2) Digital Interruptions - This is when your phone and/or computer and/or smart watch buzz and beep or chime.

The solve here is putting these devices on Do Not Disturb and turning off all alerts. You may benefit from communicating this to your colleagues so they know you'll be occupied during certain periods of time. But since our tech has a way of interrupting you for an infinite number of notifications, success requires proactively setting digital boundaries.

3) Internal Interruptions - Ay, there's the rub! You can create boundaries simply enough for the first two. But how do you handle when you interrupt yourself?

Your best bet is commit to dedicated and SHORT sprints of work to dive into a project. After handling the above two categories, all that's required is being willing to start on a given task, and committing to working non-stop for a predetermined amount of time.

PRO TIP: Having lots of trouble starting? That can be normal if you don't like the task. Long term this may be a sign you need to outsource it, as it's not in your Zone of Genius. But short term? Give yourself permission to do hilariously short periods of dedicated work. You'll be amazing how often a 5 minute session can stretch to 60 minutes once you get the ball rolling.

And if you're looking for my simplest framework for helping with the above? Go to businessforunicorns.com/book-stuff and check out my article "Time Management is About These Two Things."

Thinking Tools [Getting Unstuck]

When it comes to building your dream training gym, I'm a big proponent of goal setting and visioning work. After all, at the risk of being WILDLY reductionist, success in life is largely a matter of clarifying three things:

1. Identify where you are now
2. Identify where you want to go
3. Create (and EXECUTE!) a plan to move you from 1 to 2

Needless to say, this gets tough when your answer for #2 is "*Somewhere F*cking Else*." That's not specific enough to create a clear plan of action.

Here are a few questions to noodle on to get you thinking...

How are you planning to inspire more people to try out your core service offerings?

- Create a more compelling, higher value offer that takes all risk away from the prospect.
- Consistently tell your existing audience how you can help via your existing channels (like emails and social media).
- Experiment with a more robust paid digital strategy so more people discover you.
- Commit to personalized outreach to former clients and unconverted prospects (who already know, like, and trust you) to let them know about your awesome new offer.

How will you relentlessly improve your service week after week (after week after week)?

- Get constant feedback from your clients about how you can improve what you're doing: informally (by simply asking) and formally (by using email surveys).
- If you have a team, create standards for internal auditing your services.
- Refine and improve your service standards over time based on the above feedback.

- Identify "bright spots" so you can consistently build on what you're doing well and what your clients truly value about working with you. ⇐== This is the one most people miss!

What *other* solutions can you offer your current and potential clients?

- Develop services that complement your existing offerings.
- Design new versions of your core offering at different price points: for people with lower budgets AND those who will pay a premium for even more support.
- Think holistically about what your clients need and introduce other service providers with different expertises who they'd benefit from knowing.
- Clarify the number one obstacle that blocks client success. Then brainstorm three potential services (or products) that could solve this common challenge.

By no means am I saying you should do all these things. In fact, you probably shouldn't. This also doesn't represent a comprehensive list. But my hope is thinking through these questions may get you unstuck and thinking creatively about how to help more people.

Identify where you have leverage and take massive daily action!

You Are Not a Robot

Quick time management thought for you…

YOU ARE NOT A ROBOT.

You are a biological organism.

Now you may be asking yourself, "Mark, you eccentric f*cker, what does this have to do with time management?"

Believe it or not, it has a LOT to do with successful time management.

It's also an important consideration if you want to be a successful training gym owner.

In fact, it's a good thing to keep in mind if you want to be the best version of yourself for the people you love in your life.

Listen, you can do all the personal development in the world, and you can put forth a Herculean effort at achieving your professional goals. But… **you are not a robot.**

If you're missing the fitness piece and not taking care of your *physiology*, it's going to have a negative impact on your *psychology*. And this, in turn, will have a negative impact on your pursuit of professional greatness.

- You won't have as much energy.
- You'll be in a worse mood.
- You won't think as clearly.
- You won't be as creative.
- You'll be less resilient.

Simply put, **your physiological well-being is the foundation of your psychological well-being.**

I've worked with a lot of training gym owners over the years. And in spite of a life's calling dedicated to helping others achieve robust health, they too can often lose track of their physical self-care. In fact, it's almost cliché to see gym owners who are in poor physical shape.

The good news is, like most things in life, you'll get the lion's share of results from doing the basics with reasonable consistency:

- Getting sufficient sleep quantity and quality
- Staying active and exercising regularly and moving daily
- Eating in a way that fuels and nourishes you

For those of you NOT in fitness, I'm sorry it often seems so confusing. Much like the personal finance industry, there's a nefarious trend towards complexity that doesn't always serve the people the industry should be serving.

If you want to be successful at business, you have to take care of your body.

If you're finding yourself feeling stuck in your business...

OR simply with a nagging feeling that you're capable of doing more...

The path forward may not be reading another book or putting in more time at your desk.

It may be taking a yoga class, eating a salad, and going to bed a bit earlier tonight.

How to Learn Faster

In all honesty, I can't think of anything more fun than learning. In fact, if there's one thing I know about myself, it's this:

- *Mark Growing/Learning = Mark Energized/Happy*
- *Mark Not Growing/Learning = Mark Tired/Depressed*

Here are a few quick hits about what I'm currently doing with my education so we can be excited, energized, and happy together.

1) When you read, constantly ask yourself how you can apply what you're reading.

I am NOT a fast reader.

Part of why my pace looks so blisterin' is I consume a lot of audiobooks on 1.5x speed. But I'm very intentional about using my audiobook time for things like biographies and social philosophy. While I believe these books are very valuable to fertilize my brain, I'm usually not making tons of notes with potential action steps.

On the other hand, I usually choose books to physically read when I believe I'll get ideas for *action steps*. To that end, I read pretty damn slowly. I may only read a paragraph at a time before my brain starts to wander off and pull on some mental thread.

I don't beat myself up about this. In fact, it's kinda the point.

I'm using my morning reading time for the expressed purpose of thinking about and *working on my business*. So I take my sweet ass time, all the while making notes of action steps to take based on what I'm reading.

PRO TIP: This means you should be taking notes and transferring "To Do's" into whatever you use to capture information (e.g. notebook, document on your computer, platform like Asana, etc.).

2) If your goal for learning is better business outcomes, divide your time between function-specific principles and industry-specific tactics.

(That sentence sounds fancy, but it's a simple concept.)

Spend some of your time studying the principles of a topic.

For instance, if you want to improve your marketing, read books like *Influence* by Robert B. Cialdini and *Storybrand* by Donald Miller that are expressly NOT industry specific. You may get brand new ideas that no one else in your space is applying.

And it's important to understand first principles when considering what actions to take.

Spend some of your time studying your industry and considering potential tactics.

Look to model the most successful people in your field. Have regular conversations with your network and compare notes about what's working. Go to conferences (virtual if need be, **sniff, sniff**). Identify industry thought leaders and devour any free content they put out or pay them to get on the phone.

For instance, although much of my reading is not industry-specific, I'm a big fan of fitness industry podcasts. If you're in fitness, they're an incredible resource and fount of up-to-date information.

3) Make learning a daily habit.

While I certainly enjoy the occasional full day binge, as a rule, it's best to learn bite-by-bite. Not only does it improve memory encoding, but from a sheer numbers perspective, you'll be putting in more high quality hours.

Since I know my continued development is a mission critical activity, I personally do it first thing in the morning so it doesn't get crowded out by the demands of my day.

Want the full breakdown of how I approach learning? Go to businessforunicorns.com/book-stuff to download my entire system.

Welp. That Was Not So Good. :-/

One fateful mid-pandemic Friday night, my wife and I had dinner at a shan't-be-named Hudson Valley restaurant in a shan't-be-named Hudson Valley town.

Going out to eat is one of our very favorite things to do. And particularly during ye olde pandemic, a date night out on the town was something we desperately looked forward to all week. It also felt good to know we were supporting a small business in the hard-hit service industry. So we were excited!

And it is with great sadness that I report to you, dinner was truly *not good.*

As in... memorably bad.

(Stick with me here, there's a lesson for you and your business.)

Now here's the thing: the staff was friendly and clearly well-intentioned. Their attitude was bright and upbeat. But by my estimation, they had no idea what they were doing.

Upon arriving, they were going to sit us directly next to *the only other table seated.* This would have been strange in normal times, but all the more bizarre during the era of "social distancing."

Overall, the service was okaaay, but there was definitely a sense of "first time nerves." And I can empathize with this. Maybe they had a relatively new staff? After all, it was weird-ass times.

But the food itself varied from not good to borderline inedible, including an octopus that could have been mistaken for an actual piece of rubber (not a good sign for quality of ingredients OR cooking technique).

And nothing was more disheartening than seeing the bartender put simple syrup into literally every drink (including my Manhattan). Or asking a patron whether their Old-Fashioned was served with ice or not.

Now, you may or may not be a foodie asshole. But regardless of whether you know enough about cocktails to be slapping your forehead, I can tell you all was not well at our unnamed Hudson Valley establishment.

This makes me sad. And not because the night was ruined; Shina and I actually had a great time and laughed our asses off because it was so over-the-top poorly executed.

It makes me sad because every small business is someone's dream.

No one sets out to create a bad experience for their clients or customers. Particularly when it comes to restaurants. At some point, there was probably someone with a vision of making a living creating great experiences for their guests.

And my sense is the issue was NOT that the staff didn't care. The issue was that management hadn't created and set high standards, and hadn't properly trained the staff.

Now lest you think I'm a heartless, transplanted, Judge Judy-in' Manhattanite, this observation carries zero ill will. At a basic level, I think everyone is doing the best they can from where they are. And the staff on hand seemed to at least (kinda?) give a shit.

The lesson is that when you're in a service business, you have to:

- Create clearly documented Standard Operating Procedures
- Train the hell out of your team to execute the SOP's and
- Make sure they're consistently meeting expectations over time

One of these things went wrong this fateful Friday night.

Perhaps the owner(s) didn't know how to create good systems for service, food, and cocktails because they didn't know any better. Maybe they just opened up the restaurant on a whim.

Or maybe the owners *did* know what *they* were doing, but failed to properly train the team. It was clear that this bartender was working her first ever shift. She was soooort of being guided by another staff member who didn't seem to know much about cocktails either.

(Cue the sad, sad sound of a limpidly shaken cocktail shaker…)

The third scenario, though not in play here, can also be the culprit.

Even IF the SOP's are clear and excellent…

And even IF there's a great, rigorous training/onboarding system...

When there's no system of on-going training and accountability, standards will naturally decay over time.

So my wife and I had a good laugh at the service shenanigans, and we still had a great night.

But it reminded me that **systems, training, and management are the lifeblood of any training gym.**.

My question to you is this:

- Are you happy with your clearly documented standard operating procedures?
- Is there strong training/onboarding to ensure your staff has mastered the SOP's?
- How do you ensure the standards are being met over time?

If not, your well-intentioned team may accidentally be serving rubbery octopus and drowning whiskey with sugar. Eek!

I miss Anthony Bourdain.

If you want a simple system for creating SOP's and managing your team to stay accountable, you can go to businessforunicorns.com/book-stuff to learn more.

"Yeah, so, I Changed My Mind..."

When was the last time you changed your mind?

I hope this is something that happens semi-regularly for you. Not because there's value in changing your mind for its own sake. But because it means you're learning and growing and developing.

It's kind of amazing/discouraging how many humans get "done" growing at some point in their mid-20s. I've always been committed to avoiding that kind of stagnation.

But the price you pay for continued growth is you're going to change your mind about stuff.

For example, here's something I've changed my mind about in the past couple of years. Or, to be more precise, something I didn't properly understand/value.

If you want to be successful in life and in your training gym, you've got to get the incentives right.

If you listen to Warren Buffet's partner Charlie Munger (and believe me, I *do* listen to Charlie Munger), this is a MASSIVE element of success in any business.

This goes for you personally, for your team, for your clients/ customers, and for your society. And it's *damn hard*. Because whenever you incentivize a given outcome, you're also creating second and third order consequences.

For instance, in a famous example from colonial India, Delhi had a cobra problem. To reduce the cobra count, the British governor offered to pay people for turning in cobra heads. And... people started *actively breeding cobras* to collect the reward. Womp womp.

Furthermore, in many situations, adding incentives can backfire and actually *reduce* motivation. In particular, purely financial incentives seem to dampen creative/lateral thinking. (For more, see Daniel Pink's book *Drive*.)

However, if you have NO incentives, you don't have any influence on behaviors. No one has "skin in the game" and you're not leveraging the power of enlightened self-interest.

For instance, with your team, you want to find the right balance of guaranteed pay balanced against potential bonuses for performance. But the right balance will depend on the role, on the personality of the individual, on the needs of the business, and on finding the right performance metrics to track and reward.

This is all the stickier because you "can manage what you measure, but not everything that matters can be (easily) measured."

Of course, it's not possible to create an absolutely perfect system. But you can still create one that mitigates most of the potential downsides and captures most of the upside.

If you're not getting the results you want, ask yourself this:

- ***How are you defining and tracking performance standards for the individuals on your team?***
- ***How are you using — or can you use — incentives in your training gym to reward performance?***

It's not easy to figure out.

But since you can't opt out of human psychology, it's worth the effort!

Feedback

Here's a simple strategy that can pay BIG dividends.

You'll see better retention AND get more clarity on how to improve your services.

You see, MFF has always been good about gathering feedback. We do email surveys. We have an anonymous suggestion box. We religiously track even informal, offhand Ninja feedback in emails, texts, and conversations. We know part of our job is to find out *exactly* what the Ninjas think of their experience, and constantly look for ways to improve.

And while I've always been obsessive about reviewing these data points, for a long time I was missing a pretty obvious (and important!) form of client feedback. Now that I've streamlined my personal and professional life, I'm finally doing one of the single most important things you need to be doing as a training gym owner.

And that's consistently calling your clients.

Like… on the phone.

When you ring them, you're looking to do two things:

- Sincerely thank them for working with your business; particularly now when there's so much uncertainty in the world
- Ask them how you can improve their experience and/or help solve their fitness problems

Email surveys or check-ins definitely have their place. But you just find out different things when you actually talk to people.

There's also an obvious level of "actually-giving-a-shitness" on display when you reach out to your clients. Personally calling people can't be automated, and it doesn't scale. This very lack of efficiency is why it so clearly demonstrates real care and concern.

So this can be a powerful way to improve your relationships and increase retention.

Now if you have a smaller operation and are doing a lot of the training, you'll have an easier time keeping your fingers on the pulse. But lest you feel overconfident about your perspective, *I'd argue it's sometimes harder to see what's really going on when you're working in the business 24/7.* That's why it's so important to step out your role as "technician/coach" and put on your "business owner" hat.

Having dedicated conversations with your clients can be a great way to learn what systems are clunky and find out what other solutions you should consider providing.

There are a few different ways to slice up this pie, but the simplest way is this:

- Set a repeating weekly appointment to spend at least 20-30 minutes calling your clients
- Keep track in a spreadsheet who you call and what you discuss
- In each call:
    - Thank them for their business
    - Ask for one way you could take better care of them or improve your services
    - Ask them to share any challenges they're currently facing with their fitness goals
- Write down what you find out, and whenever possible, follow-up with:
    - Any actions you take based on their feedback
    - Content and/or solutions for their current fitness challenges

Dassit!

Now I know we've all got a lot going on. And believe me, I've been guilty of not prioritizing this in the past.

But think about it…

Is there really ANY better use of your time as a business owner than connecting with your clients, thanking them for the business, and learning how you can serve them better?

Methinks not!

Feelings

For most training gym owners, there's a direct correlation between how you *feel* about your business, and how clearly you're setting and tracking goals. If you don't have a system for setting and tracking goals, your business will feel out of control.

And if your business feels like a chaos parade, and you don't really know what's happening "under the hood," your odds of success are not good. You'll be streeeeeeessed: constantly uncertain if all your busyness is actually moving the needle. And this ambiguity has a real cost to you.

You'll show up less effectively as a coach for your clients, as a leader for your team, and as a friend and family member to your loved ones.

So let me ask the above question differently...

How <u>crystal clear</u> are your goals for this next quarter?

- Have you made those goals quantifiable?
- Are they written down and shared with your team?
- What numbers are you tracking to be sure you're on path?
- Have you broken those goals down into monthly, weekly goals?
- Do these goals guide your daily behaviors?

If not… allow me to gently remind you: "To fail to plan is to plan to fail."

Too often training gym owners find themselves feeling out of control because they're just not sure how to set and track goals in their business.

On the one hand, this stuff isn't rocket science. But in practice, I've seen it trip up gym owners time and time again. Because just like your prospective clients going it alone, it's easy to backslide, it's easy to lose sight of the metrics, and it's easy to live life reactively.

You're entirely capable of breaking out of this cycle. You CAN put in place systems that *give you deep understanding and total control* of what's going on in your business.

But it starts with you taking the action to get crystal clear on your goals for the next quarter, communicating it to your team, and holding everyone accountable to *taking action.*

Including yourself.

If you'd like access to a simple and non-intimidating overview of tracking weekly or monthly numbers, go to businessforunicorns.com/book-stuff to learn more about KPI ("Key Performance Indicator" tracking).

From Trainer to Business Owner

Let's discuss one of the most common barriers to success for the typical training gym owner:

Not updating your identity.

(Stick with me here, I know this sounds like some Burning Man bullshit.)

The skills and daily activities of a successful gym owner bear virtually no relation to the skills and daily activities of a successful fitness trainer/coach.

Sure, as an owner of a training gym you may play the "coach" role during some of your week. But the highest-leverage tasks are those that move the business forward while in the "owner" role: tracking and analyzing KPI's, creating marketing strategies, developing your team, improving your systems, etc.

This is commonly articulated as the difference between working IN your business vs working ON your business. And it's where many training gym owners drop the ball.

Sometimes there's a genuine time barrier in the way. Based on what's going on with your training gym, you may have to be on the floor a lot of the time. When you can't afford or don't have enough help from staff, you may not have many human energy hours to devote to working on the business. If this is the case, you have to fix this over time by growing your revenues and developing your team.

But some training gym owners do have the bandwidth to spend time working ON their business.

And yet they consistently procrastinate.

Like your fitness clients, you can't seem to get yourself to do the stuff you know you need to do. And for similar reasons: you just don't like (fill-the-blank for key task: marketing/sales/KPI's/etc.).

AND on some level, you don't believe in yourself. So you're not convinced it will work anyway.

I shall now say something provocative!

You don't like it because you know you suck at.

And you suck at it because you haven't invested enough time and energy studying it, getting trained and coached on it, and applying what you've learned to improve over time.

It's easy to think that successful gym owners are wired differently than you. But that's not usually true. After all, if you start out as a business person, you rarely open up a training gym. Most successful gym owners start their career as trainers.

So what's the difference?

Successful training gym owners have spent more time working on the craft of business. To put it in training terms, they've spent more time under the bar; they've gotten in more reps than less successful ones.

They start to get better over time and begin to actually enjoy the process. Because once you start to see positive results from your efforts, you suddenly don't hate it quite as much.

And most of all, because they're spending more time working ON the business – and not procrastinating by working IN the business – *their self-identity starts to evolve*. They no longer think of themself as a trainer that owns a gym. They become a business owner that owns a gym. And that flip of identity is a big deal.

It's not an easy leap to make, because your self-worth may be tied up in the positive feelings you have about being a great trainer. Furthermore, your clients may not want you to train less. They may even push back against you reducing your floor hours.

My dearest reader, I implore you to *embrace the suck*. It DOES get better. But not until *you* get better.

And while this requires discomfort, you can also shorten the learning curve. The key is not only getting in your reps, but making sure you're getting in *quality* reps.

There's no need to spend years fumbling around trying to figure it all out on your own. Find those who've done what you want to do, and learn from them. Relentlessly commit to upleveling your skills as a business owner, and I promise you, you can eventually start to like working ON your business.

And then you'll be winning at life. You'll be running a business you're proud of, helping your clients live better lives, making a great living, and most of all, *having fun.*

You can do it. I know you can do it because I did it. And I'm no better than you.

My Exact Morning Routine

I take both education AND time management very seriously. And while I'm forever tinkering with my exact schedule, I thought it may be of interest to share what I'm doing now as it's working really damn well for me.

Because if you win your morning, you massively increase the odds of winning your day.

And since I assume only a handful of you are perversely interested in the minutiae, here some immediately actionable potential takeaways:

- Going to bed and waking up at the same time every day is one of the most important things you can do for your energy levels and sense of well-being.
- If you struggle to meditate, give Vedic (or transcendental) meditation a shot. It was the first practice that clicked for me. It's had a massively positive impact on my resilience to stress.
- Drink lots of water in the first 30-60 minutes of being awake. Even slight dehydration can impact mental and physical performance. Bonus points for adding a greens formula.
- If you struggle with reading, consider listening to the audiobook version *while* reading the physical book at the same time.
- Take a few minutes to brainstorm all the things going well in your life before you dive into work. This will get you bursting with positive energy.
- Going at your day in a random fashion without a plan is not good.
- Getting overly precious and rigid in your routine is also not good.

NOTE: I believe the principles above are important. However, *I'm not offering the specific applications below as prescriptive*. I'm comfortable with a level of structure and consistency that borders on Christian-Bale-in-American-Psycho-y. Based on your current personal or professional situation this level of rigor or sheer time commitment may not even be an option. But you may see some details below that inspire exploration.

So without further ado…

Mark's Morning

Wake Up: I'm currently getting up around 6:00am - 6:45am. I set the alarm for 6:45am just in case, but usually wake up a bit earlier on my own.

One of the BEST things I have ever done for my mindset, energy levels, and wellbeing is get consistent about waking up the same time every single day. I still sleep in a bit on the weekend sometimes, but more often than not I'm up at the same time.

Meditate: I practice something called "Vedic meditation," which is essentially a form of transcendental meditation. The practice calls for 20 of sitting with your spine supported and head free. Notably, you don't try to "stop your thoughts." Instead you drop into a state of deep relaxation while gently bringing your awareness to a mantra.

The practice calls for two "sits" a day of 20 minutes each. While I rarely ever miss a day, I don't always do 20 minutes. I will also occasionally do it in the afternoon if my morning is particularly slammed. I've been doing this for years and it's been invaluable for shaving off a handful of unnecessary f*cks given.

Coffee, Greens, Water: I'm pretty hardcore about lubricating my morning, literally and figuratively. The night before I set up my coffee (mug, grinds, scale, filter, etc.), greens cup, and water bottle in the exact same carefully chosen spots. This allows me to minimize any extra movement.

Over the course of the rest of my morning routine, I'll finish 12 ounces of greens drink, 24-36 ounces of water, and two to three small (4 oz) cups of coffee. As an example of class Mark Fisher Quirk™, I drink my baby coffee cups out of espresso mugs.

Reading/Audiobooking: Once I'm settled into my reading nook in my office, I'll spend 25-45 minutes reading.

When there's an audio version available, I listen to the audiobook while also reading it at the same time. This has been a real game changer. I'm not usually a very fast reader, and I've been finding this practice has allowed me to focus even more deeply on the book at hand. Depending on the book, the speed varies wildly: as low as 1.2x for denser materials, and as high as 3x if I want to "skim." On average, 1.8x is my sweet spot.

If I catch my brain wandering, I welcome it. I often think of unrelated ideas or ways to apply what I'm reading. When that happens, I simply pause the audiobook. When appropriate, I make a note for an action step to be done later. When I'm ready to dive back in, I rewind 30-90 seconds as needed.

- I usually start with at least 15-20 minutes of personal development. Examples here include: *The Compound Effect, 7 Habits of Highly Effective People, The Gap and the Gain*, and *The One Thing*. I start the day by reflecting on how I want to show up in the world, my personal values, my commitment to service, etc.
- After that, I'll spend 15-20 minutes reading/listening to something more focused on skillset development. Specifically, leadership/management, finance, or marketing.

60-70% of my reading is re-reads of books I've already read that I want to review.

Affirmations/Gratitude Journal: This has been a habit I've long considered, but just couldn't get into it. The past few years I've gotten very consistent and I really do think it's been valuable to get my mind right. I'm usually already feeling pretty inspired from my reading; and slightly high from my morning coffee. I sit down at my desk, I read my affirmations out loud, I visualize specific elements of the life I'm creating. I take a few minutes to write down things I'm grateful for. I always start by writing out one thing I value and appreciate about my wife.

By this point, I'm bursting with positive energy to take into my morning work.

Key Priority/High Impact Tasks and Projects: I'm usually done with my morning ritual by 8:00am. After a quick review of business dashboards and my personal health habits KPI tracker, I launch into a few 30-45 minute modules of high impact project work.

These are high priority tasks that are uniquely important to move my professional balls forward. They can vary from working on presentations, preparing for a team meeting, writing marketing emails, reviewing/creating forecasts, or any number of high impact projects. The key determinant of what I choose to work on is that it must be 1) high value and 2) cognitively demanding. I start the day *crisp* and I end the day *crispy*. So I'm intentional about the time of day I schedule a given task or project.

This part of my day usually lasts till 9:30am. This is when I'll inbox zero, and if time, check in on the MFF and BFU Facebook groups.

Quick Hits About the Rest of My Day During the Week:

- **Food:** I usually eat yogurt and berries around 10am, before heading off to the gym for a mid-morning workout. I also tend to eat the same lunch and afternoon meal pretty much every day, with dinner seeing a bit more variance.

- **Training:** I strength train about 3-4 days per week, with 2-3 additional cardio workouts. I take one morning off per week, but try to be active every day..

- **Podcasts:** During my workouts I listen to podcasts, usually about the business of fitness. I find these easier to digest than audiobooks, which I now reserve for my morning reading time. Although the podcasts vary in quality and relevancy, I listen to pretty much every fitness business podcast. Most can be easily digested at 2x speed.

- **Breaktime:** 12:00-1:30pm is low energy, recharging time. This is when I cook and eat my breakfast (usually while doing some education). I pretty much eat the same breakfast every day (eggs, vegetables, yogurt, fruit, and a slice of Ezekiel bread). This is usually when I take a shower. I've been ending my showers with ice cold water at the end.

- **Afternoons:** 1:30-5:30pm is for meetings and calls with my team and clients, random work tasks, and keeping up with emails. I'll occasionally sneak in another 15-30 minute block of reading/listening. I try not to do back to back meetings when I can avoid it. I take meetings in 25 and 45 minute increments so I have "catch up" time in case meetings run a bit late and so I can catch up on some to dos as they come up. I also walk on my desk treadmill for many of these meetings. This increases my total activity and helps hit my daily step count target of 10k per day.

- **Ending the Day:** Depending on the day, I usually need 30-90 minutes to clean out my inbox, take action on small to do items that came up during my calls and meetings, and plan out tomorrow's schedule.

- **Unwinding:** Then it's time to unwind with my wife and dog before getting into bed around 8:30-9:30pm to read for a bit. I mostly read literature or hard science fiction books at this time of day.

As always, you're the person that knows your life best. This is NOT meant to be prescriptive, merely to give you ideas to experiment with.

In fact, be careful of getting overly rigid/inflexible. That can be as much of a trap as being completely reactive.

I encourage you to play with your routine over time. Discard what doesn't work. Test out new stuff, not only to improve your routine, but to keep it fresh and "alive."

5 Planning Tools

No matter the current size of your fitness business, it's important to take a moment every three months or so to step out of the day-to-day and identify how you're doing and where you want to go.

There are all sorts of models for doing this. I'm personally very partial to the book *Traction* by Gino Wickman, and we run a modified version of this with both MFF and BFU. But regardless of HOW you do it, the key thing is this:

If you don't know where you want to go, any road will get you there.

At the risk of being WILDLY reductionist, here's a game plan for building out some goals and strategies for the year ahead.

1) Personal 5-Year Vision

By choosing to start a business, you're dedicating yourself to an unconventional path. You're willing to do things that many people aren't, because you're driven to create freedom in your life and you're inspired by the creative pursuit of serving your clients.

While it's important to identify what your dream business is going to look like, you HAVE to start with your dream *personal life*. If you don't identify the specific outcomes you want for your personal lifestyle, your financial goals, your family, etc., you may create a business that's not in line with how you want to live your life.

And at that point, your clients and team are going to lose. Because martyrs don't make inspiring leaders. So you have to begin by getting honest with the life you actually want.

If you'd like a quick-and-dirty, 60-minute, 5-Year visioning exercise, go to businessforunicorns.com/book-stuff.

2) Business 3-Year Vision

It's all well and good (and encouraged!) to create a vision of your personal life that your business will fit into. But you also have to create a clear vision for the business. And once you have anyone else on your team, this particular exercise goes from "helpful" to "absolutely mission critical."

In the past, I've used and am still a proponent of the creative power of a 10 year vision for your business. But these days I think a 3 year vision is more helpful to communicate to your team where you see the business going. It's still enough time to let you dream big, but close enough for your team to see themselves in the vision AND inform the annual goals for your business.

For a comprehensive framework, check out Cameron Herold's *Vivid Vision.*

3) 3-7 Annual Goals

Once you've created a clear vision for the business in three year's time, now you can get clear on a handful of specific, measurable goals for the business for the year ahead.

These can and should be highly quantifiable metrics like:

- Total Revenue
- New Clients
- Profit Margin
- Retention Percentage

Settling on these goals is a bit of an art. They want to stretch and challenge you but still be in the realm of possibility. They should be informed by both how this year went AND where you see the business in three year's time.

4) 3-5 Quarterly Projects

In the Traction system I mentioned above, these quarterly projects/goals are called "rocks." They reflect the most important, highest priority achievements that will move your business forward to your three year vision and annual goals.

The value of identifying these projects is they prevent you from getting distracted. Having a clear priority for the quarter stops you from launching into some new project, distracting/annoying your team, and not finishing what you set out to do.

As a very simple example, let's say you have an annual goal to increase your monthly average revenue per member. There are a number of ways you could accomplish this over the course of a year. Perhaps you decide you want to offer a new revenue stream or specialty program. This could be a project to focus on during a given quarter. You would want to give it lots of attention and time and energy to ensure it's a success. And you'd also want some clear deadlines for when it should be done so it doesn't drag on forever.

This also helps your whole team get on the same page about your current priorities. Based on your business, you could potentially delegate ownership of a given project to one of your team members.

5) 5-15 Weekly (or Monthly) KPI's

Once you've got clarity on all of the above, you'll want to choose a handful of weekly (or at the least monthly) numbers to track. These "key performance indicators" will tell you and your team at a glance if you're on track for your goals and are an important marker of the business's health.

For newer fitness business owners, it's pretty normal to be flying by the seat of your pants and rely on simply looking at your bank account. But ultimately, that's a "lagging indicator." You'll want to track things like leads, conversion percentage, new memberships sold, and terminations to know in real time if you're on the path to your annual goals.

If you'd like to learn more how to do this, I've created a simple and non-intimidating guide to understanding using KPI's in your training gym. Go to businessforunicorns.com/book-stuff

****

Believe it or not, this simple structure is the bones of effectively planning the business of your dreams. Now of course, the devil is in the details. Based on the size and scale of your biz, you may need a lot more complexity.

That's why we take all members of the Unicorn Society through this planning process. Invariably questions come up. Because just like anything else in life, you won't be great at it the first time you do it.

But take heart: just like anything else in life, you'll get better over time. And there are few skills better to learn than intentionally creating the life you want!

Favorite (Free) Resource [And An Unpopular Opinion]

I'll tell ya, it's a golden age of learning for fitness business owners.

You see, when I was coming up as a personal trainer nervously making the leap to training gym owner, there weren't a ton of resources available.

Sure, I made a point to read the small handful of fitness business books available. And at fitness conferences, I was in the minority that went to see the business speakers. But "fitness business coaching" was a nascent field at the time. So much of my educational effort went into reading general business books.

Now on balance, this has served me pretty well. Many of the principles of the core functions of a business are broadly applicable.

Want to learn about marketing? Read *Influence* by Robert B. Cialdini.

Want to learn about leadership? Read *Leaders Eat Last* by Simon Sinek.

Want to learn about finance? Read *Simple Numbers* by Greg Crabtree.

You can and should read the very best business books on a given topic. But the *application* is sometimes hard to figure out for your typical training gym owner.

These days, things are a lot different than when I first got started. The Fitness Business Coaching Industrial Complex is burstin' at the seams. If you're a training gym, micro gym, or training-centric fitness studio owner, you're likely pelted on a regular basis with FB ads from gooroos.

Unpopular Opinion: This is actually a good thing.

To be clear, there are indeed varying levels of quality out there. But thanks to "content marketing", there are waaaay more resources than when I was gettin' goin'. And varying quality aside, there's unique value in hearing from people that own or work with our particular kind of business.

In particular, **fitness business podcasts are my number one source of industry specific learning.**

There's a veritable gold mine of actually useful free content out there.

You can easily learn what the entire eco-sphere of fit biz gooroos are currently recommending. I personally listen to every episode of about 15, and periodically check in on about 10 more. I can quickly compare points of disagreement between the various gooroos and guests, decide who has the better argument, and immediately go take action in our businesses and with our clients.

If you want to be successful, the fastest path requires studying business principles AND your specific industry.

(And at the risk of a shameless plug, you'll find few better resources for actionable info for training gym owners than the Business for Unicorns podcast. And while I'm promoting, you get bonus points for checking out my YouTube channel at markfisheryoutube.com.)

By all means, give Jim Collins's *Good to Great* a read.

But if you're struggling to get leads to your training gym?

Or you aren't sure how to hire your first trainer?

Or you don't know how to ask for a referral without feeling weird?

Look for the specific strategies that similar sized fitness businesses are using to succeed.

And best of all, you can find lots of great ideas for free via podcasts, newsletters, YouTube videos, and almost-free books.

Try those specific-to-your-kind-of-business strategies out first.

Then read Peter Thiel's *Zero To One* after you're at least able to pay your mortgage.

The Underappreciated Secret of MFF's Speedy Growth

There's ***one foundational asset*** overlooked by too many aspiring and established training gym owners. But first let's pop in the ol' Hot Tub Time Machine....

Back in 2011, I was a one-man band personal trainer who decided to make a real go at running an actual biz. As most of you know, things took off pretty much out the gate.

Looking back, we had a few things in our favor.

But one thing really stands out...

I knew a metric shit ton of people.

(Stick with me here, even if you don't personally know a metric shit ton of people there's a takeaway here for you...)

You see, I spent most of my 20s working regularly — and erratically — in a succession of 4-12 week acting gigs. Each gig came with a crew of 15-30ish new coworkers. Additionally, like many urban young-uns, I spent my free time hanging out, partying, and engaging in general young-person-in-NYC shenanigans.

As I gleefully ran amok all over Hell's Kitchen and Astoria and added shows to my resume, the interlapping web of showfolk got ever more intertwined.

The NY theater community is both massive AND very small. You're never more than one or maaaaybe two steps removed from anyone else.

So as a practical matter, here's the most underappreciated element of MFF's success: I just *knew a lot of people*.

Now we all know there's a limit on how many truly close friends you can have. There's also a limit on how many people you can know pretty well.

But acquaintances? No doubt there's a limit there, too. But for most of us, we're talking in the thousands.

Upon the launch of the "Mark Fisher Fitness Training & Consultations Newsletter," I wanted all my beloved people to bathe in fitness knowledge. So I loaded all their contact info into my email newsletter and started emailing irreverent fitness love letters a few times a week. And lo and behold, I had an engaged audience of humans, many of whom I actually knew from the real world.

So what's your takeaway?

The lifeblood of your fitness business is a contact database of people you *actually* know with whom you regularly communicate.

I'm not trying to make it sound like this was some master plan. When I'd head out for the evening back in the day, I wasn't thinking "Gee, this will be a great foundation of people to sell shit to one day!" I just wanted to have some laughs with pals, get weird, and potentially make out.

Nor am I suggesting you attempt to relive my glorious semi-misspent youth as a tactic to grow your biz.

What I AM saying is that the success of your training gym is largely impacted by two things:

1. The sheer number of people you know in your community (KNOW)

2. How carefully you've curated and nurtured your contact database (LIKE & TRUST)

To the first point, you can't develop relationships with people if you don't invest in meeting them in the first place (duh).

Sure, you can and should use paid digital marketing to grow this list of humans. But nothing ever replaces actually meeting people in real life. If you're an established or aspiring training gym owner, you should systematically and relentlessly get to know every other business owner in your area. Show up as a member of your community. Be friendly, be helpful, and always start your friendships with a giving hand, even if it's just showing up with free coffees.

Once you know people and get permission to stay in touch, you need to organize these contacts in a way that makes it easy to communicate with them.

I'm often amazed how many fitness businesses haven't taken the time to organize their contacts. In some cases, even *former clients* and *unconverted prospects* haven't made it to a contact list. Eek!

It's hard for people to hire you if they're not hearing from you. You're not keeping them looped in with how you can help. You can't share your offers with them. You also miss out on the chance that they may have friends who need your services.

I say again:

The lifeblood of your fitness business is a contact database of people you *actually* know with whom you regularly communicate.

Don't have one?

It won't take you that long to create. Look through your personal and professional contact list on your phone and email. Make sure they're all included in whatever contact database you use (likely an email service provider and possibly a text messaging platform). Strive to include anyone and everyone you'd say hello to by name if you saw them at the grocery store.

PRO TIP: If you're about to add in a bunch of people who have NOT been on your list, give them an email heads-up first. Let them know why they'll be hearing from you, what they can expect, and that it's perfectly ok to opt out if they're not into it.

Even if grandma won't be buying your six week challenge...

Or your best friend from college isn't in your town…

Or your wife's hilarious ex-coworker absolutely hates fitness…

If you actually KNOW these people, they'll probably appreciate hearing from you and knowing what you're up to.

And if and when they DO need help with their fitness?

Or if and when they have a friend that is looking for fitness help?

They're more likely to think of their friendly pal who communicates with them regularly and consistently.

How Many Services Should Your Training Gym Offer?

2.

Maybe 3.

Ok, great talk!

.... I kid, I kid.

Well, I'm *sort of* kidding.

I actually *do* think "2-3" is usually a good answer in many situations. But you know how I roll; I shan't leave you hanging without context!

Let's start by analyzing one of the great contradictions in any business…

Should you focus on *the one thing* that you're world class at? Should you go deeper on the handful of services that drive most of your revenue? Should you enjoy the perks of a simpler model, simpler messaging, and simpler staffing?

OR

Should you build off your reputation and offer other services to your audience? Should you grow revenue by providing other solutions that your clients need to succeed anyway? Should you go full Richard Branson and leverage your brand to start a f*cking airline??

As always, the answer is "it depends." But 2-3 service offerings is a good guideline for most training gyms.

So how on earth do so many wind up offering 17?

Time to pull out your Costco-sized tub of Vaseline and take a look at what a slippery ass slope this is.

Below are the various services a typical training gym could use as a *Core Offer*. (This is opposed to a *Low Barrier Offer*, which is usually free or at a reduced price point with no on-going commitment).

For simplicity's sake, we'll leave out variations in agreement length. We'll also ignore package size/monthly allotment of sessions, as well as how you define "small group" vs. "large group." For now I want you to focus on the sheer number of potential services and products a training gym could offer.

- 1-on-1 personal training
- Small group training (aka semi-private training)
- Defined end point 4-12 week challenge (premium pricing)
- Large group training (aka team training or bootcamp)
- Seasonal sports-specific training for high school and college athletes
- Open-gym access
- Virtual 2-way broadcast live coached large group training
- Online training with program design and accountability support
- On-demand digital workout video access

To add to this, based on your setup, you may also sell:

- Nutrition coaching
- Clothes/merchandise
- Cold case items (water bottles, pre-made protein drinks, etc.)
- Supplements
- Smoothie bar items
- Body fat percentage scans
- Equipment (bands, weights, lifting gloves, straps, etc.)
- One-off program design consultations
- Life coaching
- Workshops
- Corporate Wellness programs

Lotsa options!

So how did you decide what to offer when you initially opened up your training gym?

In reality, most of us start with what makes sense from a training perspective. Maaaaybe we check out some competitors and/or people in the industry we admire.

KEY POINT: These competitors or role models may look great on social AND be regularly missing mortgage payments. :-/

In an ideal word, we'd also consider what price points are best for our target market, our personal skill-sets, and most of all, the financial implications of that model on max revenue and margins.

Since I'm feeling magnanimous today, let's say you did all those things when you first opened up. You wound up with two main services to offer: small group and large group training. This gives you two price points and — if you run it well — two differentiated services.

You are so savvy!

But then the requests start…

CUE THE TUB O' VASELINE

Do you start offering personal training when you have two people willing to pay top dollar for it? Should you offer a hybrid training model with on-demand video workouts that could also be a potential downsell? Maybe you should go all-in and start a smoothie bar to get extra revenue and possibly drive more foot traffic? What about partnering with a local nutritionist to offer their services through your gym?

These seemingly "no brainer" additions will divide your attention. This can make life more challenging for your staff and your messaging.

(Mostly) True Statement: ***Complexity is the enemy of growth.***

And to stay simple, you'll need the courage to turn down your clients' requests when it won't work for the business.

You'll have to say no to your team when they enthusiastically bring you an idea that's too niche to really impact the business.

And on the flip side, you can and *should* stay open to other solutions. But you should only offer them if it would be a win win win for all parties. And not just for the four clients who are totally stoked about you starting a powerlifting team.

Here's a framework to consider:

- Decide how much top line monthly revenue you'd need for the new service to make sense
- Decide how much bottom line monthly profit you'd need for the new service to make sense
- Create minimum terms for survival and a deadline for hitting the above targets
- Yank the service if it doesn't meet your criteria by a certain date
- Write Mark a thank you email one way or the other

Believe me, I can understand the desire to want to take care of people AND get some extra revenue. It particularly sucks to be Dr. No with your team when they come back from a seminar with heartfelt-if-half-baked ideas.

But over time, this creeping complexity can strangle your business. And without using the above framework, you get caught thinking that you're "only a few months away" from your offering finally catching on. Plus you've already done a lot of work to build it, so why bail now? (Psychologists call this *sunk cost bias*.)

By all means, look for other solutions many of your clients need. It's appropriate and desirable to grow your revenue by selling it to them.

Just be careful you don't build a complicated business with crappy margins that confuses the hell out of your staff and clients, all the while making your business less fun.

I believe in you!

Best Market For a Training Gym (NOT What You Think)

I have a theory.

And it's *totally* upside down from conventional wisdom.

Ya ready?

"The easiest market to build a sustainable and high-margin independent brick and mortar training gym…

Is a lower population density area with medium to low average income."

I realize this flies directly in the face of what you've probably heard.

In fact, some owners will point to their success in this kind of market as proof of their business acumen as an operator.

Now your skill as an operator is of course going to be a factor. But the market you're playing in will have a powerful influence.

Here are four reasons why sometimes it's actually *way easier* to succeed in smaller markets.

(And keep reading. At the end I'll explain why big ol' markets like NYC *also* have unappreciated advantages.)

1) You won't have much (if any) competition from comparable fitness services.

There will probably be a handful of big box gym options, either globo-gym chains or independent health clubs. You may also have a smattering of Crossfits here and there. But you definitely won't have to worry about sexy boutique fitness studio chains muscling in on you. Because your market is too small.

More than likely, you'll be one of the only— and maybe *the* only— modern training gyms/microgyms. This does mean you'll have to do some education in your market to build value for your price point. Most prospects won't understand what you do, at least not at first. But all in all, this is still an advantage.

This reduced competition means retention will be easier. If clients like your service, they won't have many– if any– comparable options to consider.

2) You have less competition for time and money from other leisure activities.

In smaller markets, there's less stuff going on to take away your members' time, energy, and money. This helps support the stickiness of your service and makes it easier to build a center for your community.

To be clear, I'm not trying to make it sound like "Small Town = Bored All the Time." I promise, this ain't New Yorker shade, I swear! But it IS fair to say there's comparatively less going on.

Even if average income is lower, in practice, there's less to spend it on from day to day; at least when it comes to services/experiences. So if you create a semi-compelling service, your training gym will be an attractive option for people looking for something health-promoting, fun, and that facilitates social interaction.

And if you put in even a modest effort to create some opportunities for socializing and community, you'll have an easier time getting traction. Because you won't be competing against a robust arts scene, local professional sporting events, or the other activities that even modest sized markets offer.

3) Your business expenses will be much lower.

It's true, you may not be able to command quite as much average revenue per member or total revenue in these markets. But everything is relative.

You can get larger spaces for much lower cost per square footage. And it'll be infinitely easier to get your foot in the door and buy your own space (which is a no-brainer move whenever possible).

You'll also be able to pay your staff less money while affording them a reasonable quality of life since *their* cost of living is relatively lower. Even nominal costs for many supplies and vendors will be lower.

Taken together, these lower expenses means it's much easier to command higher margins.

(Another bonus: like your staff, *you* also live in a relatively lower cost area. That means your personal cost of living will *also* be lower as groceries, restaurants, mortgages, etc. will all be cheaper.)

4) It will be easier to retain staff.

This lower cost of living means it's easier to keep your staff around longer. Unlike mid-sized and larger markets, they won't have as many alternative fitness jobs to consider.

In turn, your staff retention improves client retention.

It also saves you time, energy, and money by reducing the frequency of job searches and onboarding new staff.

And you'll have an easier time keeping your 1-3 key hires; the roles most training gyms need to help run the day-to-day, and by extension, free up the owner's time.

Admittedly, you'll have a lower volume of options when you're looking for new team members. But the roles in a microgym don't require massive amounts of experience or high levels of unique skills. You'll still want quality humans who align with your values, but this is doable.

****

Now lest you think I'm saying there's NO skill involved in succeeding in these kinds of markets, that's NOT what I'm saying. Your skill as an operator will always have an impact on your success.

But here's some Business 101:

The context of your market can prop up a crappy operator OR make for a permanent struggle bus ride for a savvy operator.

One more point...

People always talk about how tough NYC is because there's so much competition.

I think this is *partly* right, but in important ways, also incorrect.

In fact, NYC actually has some advantages over many mid-sized markets.

NYC is expensive as hell, yes. There's always a shiny new thing to lure away clients. Competition for staff is relentless and ferocious. And much like the dating scene, many city slickers don't like to commit because they value variety and novelty.

(New York Vibes: "*You're getting MARRIED?!? But you're not even FIFTY yet! You should be out there playing the field!! Oh. Got it. You're in* an open-relationship. *Ok, cool cool...*")

However, the sheer volume is a MASSIVE strength that mid-sized markets do not have. You have a nearly endless supply of prospects. And this is a big plus over geographic areas that genuinely have a hard cap on potential clients.

Sure, you're not going to make 50% margins in midtown Manhattan. And even though I now live north of the city in the Hudson Valley, there are cheaper areas of the country for me to live. And yes, it's probably a bit more stressful because of the reasons discussed above and the generally aggressive speed of life.

But on the other hand, I don't know of any other training gym that does the revenues MFF does even in our "bad" years. So I'm not mad about a smaller slice of a pie that's literally 10x in revenue of the average training gym.

(Semi-Related Point: NYC is not for everyone, but there are hard to quantify personal and professional benefits in a city of millions of ambitious, talented, and creative people. A random hang with friends can turn into an impromptu tactical brainstorm with other multimillion dollar business owners. My personal social circle is also a constant fount of casual investment opportunities. Which I dig a lot! And while I suspect the second half of my life will be nestled in #treelife, I'm still a New Yorker till the day I die.)

Now unless you're planning to close up your business and move somewhere else, I realize this topic may not be immediately actionable.

But my hope is it encourages you to think a bit more critically: about how you look at the industry as a whole, and the opportunities and challenges in your market.

Now one more time (for the people in back)...

Your skill as an operator still matters.

Yes, you should appreciate the outsize impact of external forces on business outcomes.

But this dash-of-humility isn't a call to abandon hope or blame *everything* on your market.

If you love where you live and are committed to making it work, there's always room for a truly world-class training gym.

And disciplined execution of the basic principles will still lead to success.

Why Your Marketing Sucks (And How to Fix It)

It's ok. Don't beat yourself up!

Not all of us had the good fortune to receive a BFA in musical theater, the widely accepted gold standard for education in fitness business excellence.

Mark humbly bows to you with a flourish of his top hat

Furthermore, the confusion that leads to crappy marketing comes from a great place.

You see, you know that to achieve long term fitness success, your clients will need:

- Well-designed training programs
- Great coaches who deliver said programs
- Awesome customer service
- Education on what they need to be doing the other hours of the week
- Positive habit development
- A supportive community of peers that are rooting for them and share their values

When you ask long term clients why they stay, these are the exact reasons they'll give you.

So I understand why it can be confusing. Based on that data, it makes sense to create messaging like this:

"Come to Such and Such Fitness. We have a great community and amazing customer service (trust us). Our program design is unmatched. We also have assessments. And our team has many, many certifications!"

But when we're talking about marketing, it's important to remember you're not talking to your current clients.

Now it's not that you can't ever message the above points. But they don't exactly make your marketing message sing.

Effective marketing is about "entering the conversation going on in your prospect's mind." So we need to think from their perspective.

As I mentioned, I'm one of the lucky ones.

I'm a member of the few, the proud, and the brave...

Training gym owners with a Bachelor of Fine Arts in Musical Theater.

So this gave me an unfair advantage from day one.

(sorta kidding, sorta not.)

To be clear, I've also done plenty wrong over the years. And I'm sure I'm doing sh*t now that will have me slappin' my forehead in the near future.

But as a classically trained actor, I spent a previous career pretending I was other people. My job was to develop a deep understanding of a character. I considered their "given circumstances": what the playwright said, what the other characters said, and the imaginary world and backstory that gave life to this character.

I think this is why from Day 1 of MFF I was focused on what my friends actually wanted.

I knew what I had to deliver as a fitness professional. But when I imagined the conversation in their head, I never heard them say:

"Gee, I wish I could find trainers with a sophisticated and progressive understanding of scapulo-humeral rhythm to minimize the chances of joint deterioration as I age."

Their goals were simpler.

- Have more energy.

- Book a Broadway job.
- Get back into their favorite jeans.
- Feel confident going into an audition.
- Be stoked to wear speedos on Fire Island.
- Not be scared about getting bad news at the doctor.

They didn't really care about getting a "program."

The main thing they were looking to buy was "workouts."

"Workouts" and (gasp) "exercises."

And even then, these *features* were only their understanding of the necessary means to their desired ends: the *benefits* that they really wanted.

Of course, I knew my/our job was to deliver a great program; one designed to help them master basic movement technique and safely progress them over time.

And for them to stick with it, it had to be an enjoyable experience.

I also knew the value of community. So there had to be opportunities for them to connect with their fellow trainees and spark potential friendships.

And it had to be delivered by people who were super friendly and would ease any anxiety.

And yes, we'd have to teach them what else to do besides show up for workouts.

Ultimately, prospects need to know you, like you, and trust you enough to come on the journey you prescribe. So by all means, you can and should address the value of these elements in your education-based content marketing.

But the pot of gold at the end of the rainbow is always *the outcome they actually want*.

It's the thing they don't currently have in their life that they want support in getting.

So if you want to help your people, don't focus on the details of "flight." Help them visualize the "vacation" and smell the salty ocean breeze.

Meet them where they're at.

When you make an offer in your marketing messages, emphasize the *benefits* they want, not the *features*.

Then you can win the chance to use all your skills to take them where they want to go.

Should You Offer a Free Trial?

Let's dive head first into this hornet's nest and answer another of the most common questions in all of Training Gymdom…

Should you offer a free trial?

Here's how I suggest thinking about this…

First off, we need to appreciate that unless you have *some low barrier way* for people to "try before they buy (a big commitment)," you'll hamstring your growth. This is why "trials" are often referred to as a "low barrier offer." You need a step between "curious prospect" and "member/lifer."

And this makes sense. YOU know you're great. But even if they're a "hot" referred lead, it's only fair to let them date you before getting fitness married.

FUN FACT: Because I can be breathtakingly foolish, for a twoish year period Mark Fisher Fitness had no low barrier offer. Turns out this isn't a great way to grow your business! *Double facepalm*

The best structure for your trial will depend on your market, your avatar, your capacity, and the Core Offer your trial members will stick around for.

For most training gyms, low barrier offers fall in the following ranges:

- 7-30 days
- $0 - $149
- 3 or more visits per week
- 100% money back guarantee (if it's paid)

So how do you decide what *you* should offer?

1) If you're not getting enough leads/trials, you may need to consider lowering your barrier.

Pretty obvious point. It's easier to sell "totally free" than "discounted."

You can lower the barrier several ways (including better messaging of your 100% money back guarantee). But free will always bring in more total leads. As soon as you charge even a single dollar and get credit cards involved, you've added friction.

NOTE: If you get too many leads (good problem!), you can always change your offer and *raise* the barrier. Raising the price will usually take care of this "problem."

2) If you're doing a class/large group model, consider 1-2 free weeks.

If you have a group model, this makes it easy for people to try you out. Particularly if you have sufficient capacity in classes.

You could also consider going with 1-2 free classes. This is still attractive and will still generate leads, but your leads won't get as much exposure this way. So you'll need to make up for that with your sales and follow-up systems. Orange Theory has had a lot of success with this strategy.

3) If you're doing a higher-priced small group or personal training model, consider 1-2 free sessions.

If you run a model with a relatively higher price point per month that offers higher-touch service, a free 1-2 week offer may not be a fit. Particularly because this model really does start to run into capacity issues since you're not doing a volume play.

You could still leverage "free," but your offer will be 1-2 free *sessions*, not *weeks*. This way you can still make a free offer without giving away lots of inventory. The downside is that a single experience may not be enough time to experience the real value of this model.

Alternatively, you could make a traditional training gym offer of 28 days or 1 month of membership at a discounted rate (usually $99 or under or 50% of the regular price) with no commitment and strong 100% money back guarantee.

4) Regardless of your Low Barrier Offer, you still need strong marketing.

You can have the best offer in the world, but if no one knows you exist, it won't bear much fruit. You'll need an audience, communication channel(s), and a willingness to make a clear ask.

When you think about your marketing, you can think in terms of two buckets:

1. Value-building content
2. Offers

Whether you're using organic social, paid social, or email marketing, you want to share content that entertains, inspires, and educates. This gives prospects a chance to know, like, and trust you. Then in an ideal world, they hire you.

As you build your audience, you also need to periodically make offers with clear calls to action to take the next step: like your LBO.

5) Regardless of your Low Barrier Offer, you still need strong fulfillment and sales.

I'm lumping fulfillment and sales together, because for the purposes of the trial, there's overlap.

Fulfillment means delivering on what you've offered; give them effective workouts delivered by friendly people. Develop a personal connection and make them feel seen and cared for.

Related, an effective sales process will uncover their individual goals and obstacles. Once you know them as a human, show how your services accomplish those specific goals and solve those specific obstacles. Then make a strong offer for the best Core Offer for their individual situation.

****

Ultimately, you'll have to decide on the best path for your training gym.

And I'm not saying free offers are *always* a perfect fit.

But many training gym owners worry about tire-kickers and fear "devaluing" their services, all the while booking only a precious handful of leads each month. Believe me, "more leads" is not a cure-all in and of itself. But you certainly can't grow your biz without them.

Low lead flow is usually linked to the broader marketing strategy. But having a simple compelling offer to try you out is a core pillar.

And remember, money isn't the only cost involved. Even if they keep their wallet in their pocket, you still need to persuade them to spend time and energy. And the fear of a crappy experience sucking and/or feeling foolish.

Make it easy for interested parties to date you.

Why MFF Closed a Location [$500k Lesson]

2020 was quite a year, eh?

Got a personal story today with some takeaways for your training gym...

As a lot of you know, MFF was shot out of a cannon from the moment we hit the ground running. We hit $1m in our very first year in business. And by year four, we broke $4m in a single location.

We were bursting at the seams at our flagship location in Hell's Kitchen. And we were bumping into opportunity ceilings for our team.

After years of looking, we found a viable second location on one of NYC's most iconic streets, the Bowery.

Cut to years of challenges and difficult lessons....

First off, right out of the gate, we got screwed by our contractors. I'll spare you the details, but the mishaps went beyond the inevitable cost and time overruns. And yes, we sued. And yes we won. But you can't get blood from a stone.

When we finally opened up months and months behind schedule, we had one usable room. The rest of the 5,000 foot space was a construction nightmare. We didn't even have a bathroom on the day we opened in December of 2016. And we didn't have a working HVAC till April.

As you can imagine, this was all less than ideal. Furthermore, we were running into the inherent challenges of having two spaces. The Bowery front desk and training team (understandably) bristled at feeling left alone in an unfinished space without heat.

In retrospect, it's obvious there should have been an owner or the COO in the new space from opening to close, if for no other reason than morale. But with the lion's share of the MFF team at

HK and no finished office space, that didn't happen. While it wouldn't have solved the real issues that Bowery ultimately faced, it would have been massively helpful in preventing the Bowery team from feeling like they were going it alone.

Ultimately,, we DID get Bowery up and running. And by the summer of 2017, it was in pretty good shape. Sure, it lacked our original home's hobbled together charm. But it *was* a legit pretty-ass NYC fitness studio space; and sprinkled with enough weirdness to keep it feeling on brand.

It had its own vibe, while still feeling like the Lower East Side flavoring of MFF. And we loved our home there.

But ultimately, there were some headwinds that were going to be tough to solve.

First off, the expenses made it hard for our model to work. Not only was the rent at the top of our acceptable budget, but virtually every expense wound up being much, much higher than our HK location. Everything from cleaning to towel service to electricity cost way more. And from our current vantage point, we can see the front desk was inefficiently staffed (through no fault of the individuals involved, this was on Keeler and me).

But expenses aside, the biggest issue was this...

For all of our unprecedented success at Hell's Kitchen, we didn't really understand how to use marketing and sales to predictably grow the business.

We succeeded in our first location by being amazing at fulfillment. We had tons of word of mouth because we were damn good at delivering. And while we lacked some of the component skills of marketing, we were definitely what Seth Godin calls a "Purple Cow"; our brand was unique and memorable, even by NYC standards.

Another element that's hard to precisely quantify: we had a great location.

Well… sort of.

We were on one of the least pedestrian-trafficked streets in Manhattan. But we WERE in a neighborhood without lots of boutique facilities. We were also a stone's throw from most Broadway stage doors. And perhaps most important of all, we were a reasonable walk from Times Square and almost all of NYC's major train lines. So Ninjas that saw us (correctly) as a unique solution had a relatively easy time getting to us, even if they weren't in the neighborhood.

Now here's where a small part of me will be forever sad…

As of 2020 Q1, we finally cracked the nut of finding Future Ninjas.

We were making them attractive offers and scooping them up into our loving fitness arms. While we were only a few months into implementing our new system, we were on path to our strongest ever March.

And while HK was still getting the lion's share, it finally looked like Bowery was on a path to real, sustainable growth.

And then, well… you know. Stuff happened.

We saw the writing on the wall a few weeks into the lockdown. Unlike many operators, we bet that we were looking at solid 18 months or more before NYC inched back to normal. Sadly, we were correct.

Our Bowery landlords turned down our initial asks for rent relief. By the time they were willing to work with us, it was too late. We had decided it was best to not carry two spaces during the choppy roads ahead.

Bowery's expenses were always going to be a big haul. And it probably wasn't the ideal location for our model. But obviously a part of me feels bummed.

We never got the chance to see our growth supported by

marketing and sales strategies that *actually* worked.

Furthermore, there were many magical Ninjas we only met because we were in lower Manhattan. There were also team members for whom the Bowery Clubhouse was their primary MFF home. So this call was very emotional for a lot of humans.

But business is the art of making tough calls.

And particularly in the pandemic environment, our willingness to make tough calls *fast* set us up to build back bigger — and most importantly *better* — than before.

So here are some takeaways for your training gym...

- **Get the right contractors.** - This was the original sin of Bowery. While I'm not sure you can completely avoid bad luck here, we could have done more due diligence on who was going to do the job. We also could have sucked it up and paid more money for a more "known quantity." (To be fair, our architects, who were SUPER legit, signed off on trying this GC, but still, it was our call to make.)

- **When the market is hot, just wait.** - We came in at the top of our budget in a not-so-great neighborhood. Until recently, NYC real estate had been on fire. As a little guy, you're in a tough spot. National brands were happy to pay massive rent and lose tens of thousands every month to have flagships in NYC. This raises prices for everyone, and it makes it tough if you're trying to be profitable with your brick and mortar. For better or worse, things look to be cooled off for this next bit.

- **For the love of all that's holy, learn how marketing & sales works.** To our defense, it wasn't that we didn't know *anything*. In a lot of other markets, we probably would have been ok. We didn't balance out our (appropriate) obsession with our existing Ninjas and our team morale with focusing on actually selling shit. Many businesses have the opposite problem, so you can also go too far the other way. But looking back, it's clear this didn't get nearly enough energy or financial investment to set us up for success.

Should You Increase Rates for Long Time Members?

Yes.. Yes, you should!

Listen, I'm all about loyalty; at times, to a fault. But if there's one thing I've learned (the hard way), it's this:

When you prioritize individuals over the group, the group suffers, and then it's still a bad outcome for individuals.

This is a tough pill to swallow. Because it's a rare individual that won't be 95% focused on their immediate best interest.

Whether it be a trainer who wants special scheduling consideration or a long time client who wants to keep their pricing from five year ago, the individual will not appreciate your loyalty to the business at large. They can't see the second and third order impacts of prioritizing their needs over the needs of the "organism."

And this suuuuuuucks.

But alas. You decided to open up a training gym.

So you get to learn fun/painful things!

Now to be honest, I love *the idea* of honoring your most loyal members. After all, they've stuck with you. Shouldn't they receive some benefits?

Totally. They should get oodles of love and care. Too many training gyms spend their time chasing prospects without constantly working on their relationships with their long term members. You should actively look for ways to honor and reward long term commitment.

However, *they still need to pay you more money as costs increase.*

Because your landlord isn't "rewarding your loyalty" as a tenant by keeping your rent the same year over year.

Your team is not "rewarding your loyalty" as an employer by never expecting a raise.

Your vendors are not "rewarding your loyalty" by keeping their prices static on all the products and services you purchase.

The cost of business will go up year over year. And you'll need to increase your rates or you'll get in an ugly jam; particularly if your business makes it to 5-10 years and beyond.

(Perversely, the one way this *could* work is if you have horrible retention. But that's a whole other issue.)

Now, gentle reader, come sit on Papa Mark's knee to learn of another blunder of yesteryear...

The reason I feel so strongly about this is because I made this same mistake myself (read: loyal to a fault). When we opened MFF, we were committed to never raising anyone's rates. But as we approached our sixth year, it was clear this wasn't tenable.

Not only was our original pricing structure pulled out of our butt (read: *not actually that profitable*), but over time, our costs continued to increase. And since our retention has always been unusually strong, even with an influx of new members paying higher rates, our average revenue per member wasn't growing fast enough to keep up with our increased costs of doing business.

Furthermore, it made our back-of-house a total administrative nightmare. At one point we had something like 40 plus (!!!!) different active memberships. This had massive costs in complexity and time — and therefore money — to manage all these different options. It also created lots of opportunities for back-of-house mistakes (and pissed off Ninjas) when we needed to adjust billing.

So in the summer of 2016, we ripped off the band-aid. And YOWZA, it stung.

We wanted to honor the terms of our original agreement. And since Ninjas had made the commitment with the expectation that they would keep their rates forever, we didn't want to hold them to auto-renewing agreements since we changed the terms.

(Yes, our contracts DID say we could raise their rates. But that wasn't the social compact we had made. So that would have felt crappy.)

In order to "delay the pain," we gave our members a heads-up in July that rates would go up in the new year. Since our oldest members were now seeing pretty significant increases, we also offered some of them discounts for the entire following year. Finally, we asked Ninjas to sign new agreements to confirm their understanding of the new world. In practice, we were letting everyone out of their agreements.

All in all, there wasn't actually too much pushback. We weren't forcing anyone into the new rates, we gave them plenty of time to emotionally adjust, and we also offered discounts to those seeing the steepest hikes.

But by asking all Ninjas to "re-sign up" for their membership, we saw a massive dip in members for a six month period.

In MFF lore, we call this period of time **The Red Wedding.**

Ultimately, we obviously sorted it all out.

But the amount of time and effort that went into making the change AND the short term hit to revenues was not fun.

I rarely speak in absolutes, but I will here:

If you're attempting to reward loyalty to your members by never raising their rates, *you're making a mistake.*

Unless you're committed to truly terrible year-over-year retention, the math just doesn't work.

Will your members love it? No. Of course not. But they'll get it.

Raise your rates every single year just like every other business in the world.

Mental Health & Owning a Training Gym

If you own a brick and mortar training gym, micro gym, or fitness studio, the pandemic was not the easiest time.

To be fair, the pandemic was not easy for *anyone*. But for obvious reasons, your business has been more stressful than usual.

And even in the best of times, running a training gym is no walk in the park.

Even in normal times, competitors and trends come and go. Your approach to growing your business needs to keep adapting year after year. The market never stops changing. You're constantly balancing the needs of the business, your team, and your clients. You need to decide how to allocate your time, energy, and money. All the while, you'll invariably face criticism; some will hurt because it's unfair, and some will hurt because it's spot-on. You're hoping to eek out some time for yourself and your loved ones and maybe even take some days off once in a while. And of course, you're hoping to actually take home enough income to justify the stresses of being a business owner.

Now if you're like me, you wouldn't have it any other way. But let's be honest, it's going to take a toll sometimes.

I can say I've never been so depressed in my life as I was in the weeks when the world first shut down.

Ultimately I bounced back. But it was roooough going for a bit.

Part of my lethargy was complete exhaustion from a (thankfully moderate) case of the virus.

And part of it was because it felt like the walls were closing in.

Because when you run a business with your whole heart, it's only natural to get a wee bit over-identified with the business. And after an awesome first 10 weeks of the year, it was devastating to see everything at risk.

And of course, NYC was not the easiest place to live in March and April of 2020.

I did my best to keep up with emails, but I was not my usual self. As my body fought off the sickness, I was sometimes taking two naps per day. I compulsively doom scrolled on my phone, anxious about whatever bad news was coming next.

And all the while, my cherished 30th floor view of Manhattan gave me a clear view of a ghost town. New York City's hustle and bustle was replaced with a single unwelcome guest: the ever present sounds of ambulance sirens.

I share this with you not for sympathy. Because even in the worst of it, I had it much, much better than many people who've had their lives completely turned upside down.

And while many difficult decisions had to be made for MFF, ultimately the business survived and thrived. And I don't take that for granted. Many fitness businesses didn't make it.

While this is an extreme example, here are some things to consider if you're looking to improve your headspace.

Get support from other people

Certainly if you're in a supportive partnership or can confide in close friends, that's a powerful salve. But I think more formal support is necessary if you want to perform at your highest levels.

Depending on your situation, it could be hiring a life coach. It could also be periodically speaking with a therapist.

Having a formal group of other business owners is also key. These groups are often ostensibly about helping your business. And a good coaching group should deliver value on that front. But there's also specific magic in a like-minded community of people who face similar challenges.

I can't imagine this past year without my Entrepreneur's Organization small group forum.

And many of our members have said the same about the Unicorn Society.

Get serious about time management and "winning the day"

One of the challenges of running a training gym is the volatility. And there's always going to be a lot you can't control; you find out a key employee has been training clients on the side, your landlord suddenly jacks up your rent on your next lease, your Facebook ads go from nailing it to snailing it overnight, etc.

The way to handle these slings and arrows is to control what you can control.

Good time management practices help you set up each day as a "game you can win." By planning quarterly priorities and meticulously time-blocking each day, it's possible to feel accomplished. The outcomes are never 100% in your control. But you'll feel better about life if you're taking ownership of consistently executing your inputs.

If your life is a parade of chaos, you should commit to learning this skill. Not only will you get better results in your business (and relationships), but you'll feel more grounded.

Take Care of Your Fitness

I don't know anyone running a training gym who hasn't fallen off on their own fitness at times.

And like any human, it's perfectly ok to have seasons of grinding where you can only manage your minimums. But too many training gym owners get into a permanent routine of barely training, skimping on sleep, and eating crap and drinking too much to self-medicate.

Your brain is biological. Part of maintaining your mental health is putting in the right physiological inputs. And lucky you… you know what to do already! :-)

I admit, as a young man, much of the motivation behind my fitness was vanity. As a not-quite-as-young-man, my primary motivation is my mental performance, energy, and a positive mindset. And that doesn't happen without consistent exercise, nourishing food, and high quality sleep. Bonus points for adopting a meditation practice.

****

I heard a great metaphor once for entrepreneurship:

It's like riding a lion like a surfboard.

Everyone looks at you and thinks...

"WOW! That person is riding that lion like a surfboard… so cool!!"

Meanwhile, you're all like…

"HOLY SHIT!! How did I get up here?? Eek, I'm riding a lion like a surfboard!! OMFG!! I better not slip! Holy shit, WTF!!!"

Yep. Running a training gym is not for the faint of heart.

But if you're like me?

If some depraved and twisted part of you actually *enjoys* the challenge?

I hope you can apply some of the above strategies to take an edge off the emotional downsides.

Should You Have Your Prices on Your Website?

The Fitness Business Thought Leader Industrial Complex has many strong — and conflicting — opinions on this topic. Here's my personal take.

In a vacuum, your best bet is often something like this:

"Prices start at X, but depend on what customized plan we create for your goals. [CTA for them to find out more]"

Now let's add some context to consider....

This middle ground is a great way to go, as you'll get *some* pre-qualification, but you're doing so with your lowest price. If people are disgusted by your cheapest offering, it stands to reason they may not be a fit.

This move is also helpful when you have complex membership offerings that could be daunting at a glance.

Speaking of, if you're a training gym with lotsa lotsa options:

- Stop it. Kill your darlings. Complexity is the enemy of growth (and happiness). I get why this "creep" happens. Your clients will always ask for the exact variation of services they personally want. Your job is to politely and kindly tell them "no" if it's not best for the business as a whole. You just can't be everything to everybody. And you can't have a thousand membership options. Unless you like to make your business confusing and annoying to clients and staff alike.

- If you INSIST on having lots of options, at least you won't confuse and horrify prospects by showing your Quantum Physics-complicated rate sheet. You can simply make your prescription in the Strategy Session/Discovery Call once you know their goals, preferences, budget, time constraints, etc.

But what if you have a relatively simple set of options? Does it make sense to show your prices on your website then?

Maybe. However, the typical modern training gym is going to be more expensive than Planet Fitness. And since most prospects will first look to price, sometimes you'll miss the chance to show the value of what you do.

Sure, the people that come through will (in theory) be more qualified. But you may be missing the chance to help other people who ran away after seeing your pricing.

You may be tempted to go this route if you're "getting too many tire kickers." But more often than not, lack of pricing transparency is why you feel you have "tire kickers." If you're getting lots of people turned off by price, it means you're not good at building value in a sales conversation.

Very few people are actually tire kickers. Even with a low barrier offer, they still pay the price of time, energy, and face the potential that you suck.

True, some people may legitimately not be able to afford your services. But if you could actually analyze their yearly spending?

Here's what the data would say most of the time:

They absolutely have the discretionary income. But they value other things more than your services.

Ok, well in that case, should I just not mention price at all (outside the free or low cost Low Barrier Offer/Trial)?

Maybe. But many prospects will feel annoyed if they can't get a ballpark idea of your pricing.

So this is essentially the inversion of having your rate sheet on your website: you won't scare anyone away based on price, but the lack of transparency may also turn people off.

For what it's worth, this describes your faithful penpal Mark. I'm a wildly impatient person, so if I don't see pricing on a product or service, I will almost always bounce.

That said, even here, if I reeeeally want the product or service and the company has built sufficient value via content marketing, I'll likely still reach out. So based on your market and services, this can also work.

Ok, got it. Maybe I just split the difference and go with "*Prices start at X, but depend on what customized plan we create for your goals. [CTA for them to find out more]?*"

Oh my gentle reader, how I marvel at your insightful analysis!

Final point:

Many of your prospects won't spend that much time looking at your website anyway. So whether your prices are on there or not, you'll need to expect a fair number won't have any context for pricing when they come in to discuss membership options.

So while you can test the above options, the biggest piece of your success will be how skilled you are at building value and making offers in your sales conversation.

You'll Never Be Done

We recently did our quarterly planning session for Mark Fisher Fitness. This is a full day meeting where the leadership team get on the same page about the next three months.

As usual, it was a long ass day. But also as usual, we ended the day feeling organized. Orderly. Focused. These planning days always create a lot of clarity.

Importantly, this kind of planning gives us permission to NOT worry about all the other stuff for the next three months.

But here's what I want you to appreciate: we still have an enormous list of unsolved problems and opportunities we aren't acting on.

You see, when you run a business, you never get "done."

This can tough if you're overly goal-directed and achievement oriented (*Mark sheepishly raises his hand*).

You will always have problems.

The only time your business has no more problems? After you've shut it down and settled up all remaining obligations.

Now some problems are more desirable than others.

For instance, hiring new team members to keep up with demand is better than your revenue tanking.

But unless you periodically take a step back, it can be easy to lose perspective. It can be easy to feel overwhelmed and not appreciate even "good problems." This has been truer than ever during the last year, where things have changed very quickly and planning has been difficult.

So let's say it again...

Your business will always have problems.

That's why taking time to step out of the day-to-day is so important. It lets you see the big picture, organize the many issues vying for your attention, and make decisions about where you're going to focus. And where you're NOT going to focus.

And then…

EXECUTE EXECUTE EXECUTE.

And after another 1-3 months, rinse, wash, and repeat.

And another bonus? If you're doing this in a systematic way, you'll see evidence of forward progress by reviewing the challenges you've solved and projects you've completed. And that too can build momentum.

Number One Missing System

Today I want to highlight the most common missing system I see in training gyms and microgyms...

And that's the *follow-up*.

Let's assume you've got...

- A compelling low barrier offer that makes it easy to get started and removes all risk
- Communication channels to make that offer (email list, paid digital, texting prospects, asking for referrals, etc.)

If that's the case, you're going to be getting leads. Some of these are hot leads referred by existing clients. Some of these may be relatively colder leads coming from paid digital marketing. But regardless, there are people raising their hands that are interested in what you're doing.

Now what?

This is where the magic happens.

Or, all too commonly, this is where the magic does NOT happen.

First, real talk: many training gyms don't have a good LBO and/or don't communicate about it enough to get traction. If you don't have this in place, you won't be getting many leads. So you want to solve that first.

But assuming that's in place and leads are coming in, the vast majority of training gyms do minimal to any follow-up.

When an inquiry comes in, they'll maaaybe respond with a single email that answers any questions, often lacking a clear CTA for next steps.

They won't ask for a phone number, so they can't call them or text them back, even though most people prefer texts to email.

And there's no system to continue to follow-up over time if they don't hear back.

They may not even put their contact information into their email database, so the lead gets no long term nurture via regular value-building email content.

Even worse, many owners fail to follow up because they "don't want to be annoying." This is in spite of the fact that we're talking about a human who has explicitly opted in and/or reached out with interest in doing your low barrier offer.

YIKES.

Now I have empathy here. Particularly for smaller training gyms, there's always a lot going on. You're likely coaching sessions, managing your team, and handling your current clients. So I get it.

Nonetheless, if you have any interest in growing your business, or simply not shrinking over time due to attrition, you NEED to have a follow-up system in place.

This can look differently based on your capacity and how much you want to automate. But it's worth knowing most people don't buy till the **5th to 12th outreach**. (!!!!!)

Here a few best practices to implement:

- Decide on your follow-up pulse and length. For most training gyms, you're looking at 5-14 days, with more frequent follow-up (usually daily) in the beginning.
- Follow-up via different channels. Use a phone call, send a text, and send an email.
- Acknowledge that you're going to keep following up because the individual said they were interested. Be a human and not a weird sales robot.
- Send them content that can help them learn more about what it's like to work with you. Bonus points if it's personalized based on their stated goals.
- Use video texts. Most people will assume your emails and

texts are automated. To break through this, be *extra* human and personalize your outreach a much as possible.

- If you haven't heard back, make a note to follow back up again in a few weeks. Do this forever.
- Add their email to your email database so they get your regular value-building email content (including offers for what to do next if they want to work with you). Sometimes it will take them a few months — a few years – for the timing to be right. Play the long game.

Does the above feel a bit much to you? I get that. The last thing you want is to be pushy.

I'm all for respecting people's autonomy, but here's the thing to keep in mind...

They reached out to you for help.

They actively expressed interest in your services.

It's not like you're spamming a cold list you purchased from a broker. These are real live humans who reached out to YOU to learn more.

Yes, for many of them, life will come up. Maybe now isn't the right time. And of course, if they do respond and let you know that's the case, you'll stop following up (at least until the time you've mutually agreed upon for you to circle back).

And most of the time when you DO make contact?

They'll usually thank you for your continued outreach.

Think of your follow-up pulse as the beginning of your coaching relationship. It's a reflection of your dependability, dedication, and commitment to their success.

One of My Biggest Oversights

Let's discuss something I could have done better during MFF's *first 9+ years*.

You see, I will forever identify as an artist. I want MFF to be the most human business possible. I don't want to overly constrict our operations by forcing people into the straight jacket of systems that leave no room for humanity.

And when it comes to our processes, we've actually done a pretty good job overall. Our standard operating procedures have evolved. And of course we have some holes we're working to fill. But many of our core systems have been bearing fruit for years. For instance, our Snatched in Six Weeks program is super dialed in and reliably gets amazing feedback and consistent results. Every time. For ELEVEN. YEARS.

But you know where we/I have been shitting the bed?

Running our business by the numbers.

In retrospect, we got away with a lot of bullshit because we were so good at fulfillment. And because of that, I didn't have the complete mastery of data and numbers that is now my daily obsession.

Sure, I knew we were making a profit. And I knew we had lots of happy Ninjas and our survey scores were great. But most of my attention was on the mission, the values, and the culture.

You see, pretty much every book I read said *this* was the important thing. After all, I didn't want to be an evil corporate person. I mean, I read Simon Sinek books for feck's sake... I stand for the LIBERATION OF HUMANITY. I rage against your soulless capitalism-as-cancer approach to business!!!

What I didn't realize is I was over-correcting for a problem I didn't personally have.

I didn't realize Simon Sinek writes for a mid-level manager at a Fortune 500 oil company who really does want to extract every dollar possible out of every professional interaction.

In other words, Simon Sinek was NOT writing for a musical theatre actor turned entrepreneur who was prone to anxiety if anyone on his team or among his clients was anything other than existentially fulfilled by their relationship with business he founded.

Say what you like about the many imperfections of MFF or yours truly. But you definitely can't say we were focused on the bottom line above all else. (I mean… you *could* say that, but I'd laugh my ass off). Nor were we uncaring when it came to our team's feelings or desires. And every time we got a negative piece of feedback from a Ninja, I took it to heart, seeing what we could change.

And from this vantage point, I see we lacked balance. We were TOO focused on the feelings and the art and the soft stuff.

Yes, this stuff absolutely matters. And if I have to choose, I'm always going to bias towards humanity and generosity.

And if you ONLY focus on your COGS (Costs of Goods Sold)? Or week-over-week increase in conversion percentage, or cost per lead, or lifetime customer value, or customer acquisition costs? Also bad. No heart = bad.

BUT!

You need *both*.

And I can honestly say I've learned more about running a numbers-based organization in the last year than I did in my previous nine years combined.

While we're still not perfect, every single person on our team has 1-3 numbers we track for performance. We are very transparent about what we're tracking and make it clear that hitting minimums is required to stick around. Pay raises are based on consistently exceeding expectations. They do not automatically happen. Sure, we'll consider more subjective stuff too. Numbers can be gamed. And not everything that matters can be (easily) measured. Values-in-action still matter too.

But having no numbers for your team performance = bad. Performance assessment becomes *entirely* subjective. This means it's easier to get tricked by bad actors and politics and miss who is producing real results in your business.

Furthermore, I keep a careful eye on the percentage of revenue going towards various expenses. And all those fancy numbers up there? COGS, CPL, LTV, CAC, KFC, etc. etc.? I'm looking at them pretty much every single day.

Because if you REALLY care about the feelings and experiences of your team and your clients, you HAVE to know this stuff.

It doesn't matter if you don't like numbers. This isn't hard math. You have to *learn* to like it, or at the very least, tolerate it. If you don't, you're committing malpractice.

You can't tend to the spiritual and emotional needs of your team and your clients if you burn out because your margins are so bad you're making $7 per hour for your 80 hour workweek, all the while not seeing your kids grow up.

And you sure as hell can't help anyone if you close your doors because you're not tracking even basic numbers for your business's health and an unexpected expense leaves you choosing between rent and payroll for your team.

I'm very passionate about this because I know how much order and piece of mind — and fun! — it can bring to your business when you break it down to trackable behaviors and outcomes.

If you're not sure where to start, keep it simple.

For a high level overview of tracking numbers, head to businessforunicorns.com/book-stuff and download the bonus guide for this book.

How Much Should You Charge for Your Services?

I want to give you some (very crude) rules of thumb for what you should charge at your training gym.

But first, let's acknowledge this fact: most training gym owners undercharge for their services.

This often comes from a reasonable place.

First of all, many training gym owners are nervous about getting price objections. After all, won't keeping prices low lead to more volume?

Well… sort of. But I like Seth Godin's take here: you'll know you're at the correct price point when 20% of people are offended by your pricing.

The reality is you will ALWAYS get price objections. Particularly if you're in a market where the other options are low priced, volume gyms where people rent access to equipment. Now we know that's not a fair comparison; you're not selling equipment access, you're selling coaching and accountability. And part of the job of your marketing is to make it clear that you're totally different solutions. But this is likely to still happen once in a while.

Also of note: different people just value different things. Some people are relatively self-sufficient at the gym and like doing their own thing. And some people just want to spend money on other stuff because they value it more than what you have to offer. The better you get at building value for what you do, the less this will happen. But that's just the way this is going to go sometimes. And it shouldn't make you concerned that your prices are too high.

In fact, I don't think I've EVER even seen a training gym that was genuinely having issues because its prices were too high.

("You know, we were having all sorts of struggles making our rent each month. But then I lowered my rates, and now we're burstin' at the seams and more profitable than ever!" - Literally no one ever)

The second piece is stickier. A lot of training gym owners run smack dab into their own feelings of self-worth. While I can't do this justice here, if you don't believe your services are actually worth $XXX, it's going to be very hard to charge that much and/or successfully sell at that price point.

So assuming you are truly awesome at what you do… how much *should* you charge?

Different markets vary a bit, but a lot less than you'd think. The real consideration is the value of the service you offer, and the costs to fulfill that service.

I do think it's ok — and even wise — to look at what your competitors are charging for comparable services. But it should NOT be the final consideration when you're determining what to charge.

You need to consider what's realistic for your market, but you also need to build your model backwards: in other words, look at the cost of fulfilling your services and make sure you can run it profitably after paying your overhead. As a rule of thumb, a typical training gym should shoot to keep total expenses no more than the 60-70% of revenue.

In practice, most don't. This is partially because they don't control expenses that well. But the bigger issue tends to be they were under-priced from the get-go and designed to fail.

Most training gym owners look at comparable solutions in their market, then set their prices lower. If the owner ran numbers beforehand, they figured on a best case scenario for anticipated volume and for expenses, assuming nothing goes wrong and nothing breaks. This means they charge the absolute smallest amount possible in an attempt to not get price objections and/or butt up against the limits of their personal belief in their own self-worth and the value of what they do.

So at the risk of being laughably crude…

If you run a higher volume, large group class model (15 clients or more per session), you should be charging an average of at least $175/mo., ideally $200/mo. or more.

If you run a higher touch, small group personal training model (4-6 clients per session), you should be charging an average of at least $300/mo., ideally $350/mo. or more.

You don't need 500 clients to do well at these price points. And if you have less clients paying a higher average monthly rate, you can provide much, much better service.

You can afford to keep your space in better condition.

You can afford higher quality staff and keep them around longer by paying them actual living wages and even offering benefits.

You can afford to spend some money on marketing so prospects find out you exist.

You can afford extra service bells and whistles so you can treat your clients as unique and individual humans.

And you can afford to pay yourself an income that's appropriate for the value you're creating and the stress and risk you incur as a small business owner.

Now all of this is predicated on you being awesome at what you do. I honor the introspective part of you that is wondering if you can really justify charging these higher rates. Because it means you genuinely care about a fair exchange of value with the clients who are trusting you. Believe me, this is a valuable quality and you rock for thinking about this!

But at a certain point, if you're looking to make this a sustainable career with a sustainable training gym business, you've got to develop both your skillset and confidence to the point where you're comfortable with these numbers.

How Can I Make Sure My Team Follows Our Systems?

Whether you've got a larger facility with 10+ staff, or just hired a part time trainer and/or admin, the only way for you to have true peace of mind is with a well-trained team.

The first step on this path is having good ***systems***: clearly defined standard operating procedures (SOPs) that lay out exactly what should be happening.

Whether it's opening the space in the morning, cleaning the bathroom, or conducting a training session, good SOPs provide crystal clarity on exactly how things should go. This means balls don't get dropped, and clients get a consistently awesome experience.

Once you have SOPs, the next step is making sure you've properly trained your staff. You can have the best SOPs and team in the world, but if they haven't been trained, it's going to be hard for them to translate your systems into execution.

Writing SOPs and training your team are each big topics in and of themselves. But assuming you've got that down, let's discuss a few strategies for making sure your team is able to perform.

First, if it's possible to use a written checklist and/or follow-along video, you should. A lot of tasks don't need to be done in real time with a client: closing down the facility for the night, resetting the training space, handling an emailed membership request, etc. This allows your team the luxury of referring to a checklist to make sure they get it right every single time.

However, some tasks won't work like this. While it may be ok to refer to the program when coaching a session, many of your coaching standards need to be memorized.

Likewise, you'll want a script for sales conversations (which is really just a specific set of SOPs). But it would be super awkward and clunky to read off the page while chatting with a prospect.

And you'll need to train your front desk how to handle negative feedback in real time. Because if they ask a fuming client to wait while they look for the written checklist, the encounter won't go well.

Here are four ways to ensure your team has mastered your real-time SOPs:

1) Written Quizzes

Being able to pass a written quiz doesn't necessarily mean they'll be able to execute in real world conditions. It's possible to *know* what to do, but not be able to deliver. But if they haven't even committed the system to memory, they won't magically do the right thing in the moment.

2) Role-play

Most team members don't enjoy role-playing. It will feel awkward. But do it anyway. This is the best way to make sure your team can execute. The more important the system, the more often you need to role-play. For instance, in an ideal world, sales role-plays happen every day.

3) Feedback from Clients

This can be leveraged two ways. First, you can usually learn things in the course of your regular feedback collection. Even asks for general feedback can help uncover if systems are being followed correctly.

Second, you can actually handpick certain clients and ask for their help in looking for very specific feedback. This could be asking them to keep an eye out for a particular behavior you're looking for, then circling back to them to collect their assessment. This functions almost like micro-secret shopping from existing clients.

4) Have Your Team Audit Each Other

This approach can be a double whammy. By having your team audit each other (in real time or via recordings if need be), you'll give your audited team member another chance to get feedback. Additionally, *the auditor* will deepen their mastery of the system being audited and make sure it stays fresh in their mind.

Remember, this all starts with having a system in the first place. But that's only the first step.

By applying these strategies you'll know your team is consistently delivering the goods for your clients!

Fitness Business Coaches [The Truth]

Here's a common point of debate in the Fitness Business Guru Industrial Complex:

Do fitness business coaches need to be running their own training gym?

One side of the issue says:

"Yes. If you're not (currently) running a gym, you don't really know what's working now. If you don't have a gym, at best, you're talking about things that worked when you had a gym, and at worst, you're blowing hot air about theory. Furthermore, if you're so good at the business of fitness, why can't you figure out how to run/keep your gym going with a team to do most of the work anyway?"

The other side of the issue says:

"No. Star players in a given sport are not necessarily great coaches. You need to know how to *coach*. Besides, principles are principles. And if all you do all day long is coach training gym owners, you'll know as much — if not more — than a part time business coach who's also busy running their own training gym. In fact, if you're *really* great at coaching gym owners, you should be all in on it and give it (and them) your full attention and energy."

Let's first start by saying an uncomfortable truth:

Once you understand the basics of marketing and sales, it's arguably easier to make a living coaching training gym owners than by actually owning and running a training gym.

Between the minimal overhead expense and complexity, to the higher average monthly revenue of business coaching versus fitness coaching, this is the perverse reality.

Over the past several years, we've seen the rise of an endless sea of Fitness Business Gurus speaking to brick and mortar training gyms and micro gyms. A handful of these coaching companies have reached multiple seven and even eight figures in a blisteringly fast amount of time. Furthermore, the sheer volume of Gurus in the game has exploded.

So what's going on here?

Here's a theory...

Many training gym owners with a profitable (or in some cases, *unprofitable*) gym discover they can make another $5-10k in (almost all-margin) monthly revenue by hanging out their shingle as a Fitness Business Coach. In smaller markets, this can mean a massive percentage increase to their take-home income. In many cases, achieving a comparable increase in take-home income would be nearly impossible in their training gym.

Many of these same gym owners begin to do the math and realize (not incorrectly) that they can skip all the headaches of running their brick and mortar and just double down on their business coaching offerings. This means they can spend more time at home with family, skip the early mornings and late evenings at the gym, travel more, and live anywhere they want. So they "sell" their business; this is generally a fancy way of saying they liquidated their equipment costs and got out of their lease in exchange for some cash from an employee or a client who will take the joint over.

In some markets, the owner is able to keep their gym but step out of the day-to-day by finding a proxy. They can pay a general manager and/or a head fitness coach to take over most of the operations in exchange for a higher salary and/or profit share. After all, the owner has a growing side hustle, which lets them be more generous with paying out work in the training gym.

Let's be clear... no judgement over here. All of this makes sense.

Any successful training gym owner will find themselves as interested in business as in fitness, if not more. They develop a genuine passion. It's only natural for them to want to share what's working and help other owners, AND to explore ways to spice up their work life and make more income. It's nearly analogous to the path they took as a trainer-turned-owner excited by the opportunity to be paid to share their passion for fitness.

Furthermore, many owners will not want to run a single training gym forever. They will get bored. They will crave new challenges and the opportunity to make more income. Based on their skill sets, lifestyle preferences, and location, being a business coach is a much easier way to go than multiple facilities, franchising, or licensing. And as per above, there are many lifestyle benefits when compared to actively operating a modest-sized training gym.

Once again, I'm not poo-pooing any of this. I'm just pointing out where the incentives are.

So what's the deal here?

Do you *need* to own and/or run a training gym to be credible as a fitness business coach?

Let me first say... I run a successful training gym and also do business coaching. The same is true for BFU coaches Michael Keeler (my business partner in both businesses) and our fellow BFU coaches Pete Dupuis and Ben Pickard.

And I do think there's a unique value in talking to people that know what you're going through in real time. Particularly during the pandemic, training gym owning business coaches had a unique and visceral shared experience with their clients.

But do I think you *have* to currently own a training gym to be successful?

Does it *require* having your own facility as proof of your acumen and to use a petri dish to test out strategy?

No. I don't think that's necessarily true.

Yes, there are many unqualified people that couldn't hack it as owners who became coaches. But there are also super legit people who know what they're talking about and no longer care to own a gym themselves.

And just because someone is currently running a gym doesn't mean they're instantly credible. It doesn't prove their gym is very profitable. Or that their success isn't a function of being in a less-competitive market.

However, it IS appropriate to acknowledge the incentives. When deciding if someone's formal paid or informal unpaid coaching is credible, their current status (and previous history) as a gym owner is certainly worth factoring in.

Because you do want to keep an eye out for the less-than-qualified coaches who "sell" their gym to bravely pursue their personal legend of blahblahblah because if I can help training gym owners, I can multiply my impact by helping them serve their clients better and then I can achieve my mission to PERSONALLY SAVE THE WORLD here go ahead, drop into my Clickfunnels and get on a sales call and sign up for my mastermind but warning this isn't for *everyone* action takers ONLY.

Ok ok... I'm poking fun!

Listen, I personally love owning a gym AND being a business coach. Yes, I think it gives some valuable real-time perspective. But I see advantages to both and I think people should do what they want with their life.

AND training gym owners should also decide if and how this factors into their decision making when hiring someone to help them.

Can You Sell Your Training Gym?

Probably not. At least not for a lot of money.

In entrepreneur circles, it's often suggested you should build your business with an exit in mind. After all, most people won't want to run their business forever. It makes sense to have a plan to cash out. In fact, many businesses are built specifically with the goal of creating an asset to sell.

However, rare is the training gym that runs totally smoothly with minimal input from the owner. And in the event that it does, there's usually a high level of risk for a potential buyer, as invariably there's a key employee running the show. And if this employee leaves the business, the owner will likely need to step back in as operator, and/or expend time and effort searching for and training a replacement.

Usually when an owner sells a training gym, it goes best when it's sold to an employee (usually the key one functioning as the operator) or an impassioned client who loves the business.

An outside investor looking to own the business as an asset may be willing to pay *something* for the membership base, lease, equipment, existing systems, etc. But unless it's being sold to an employee or client, the buyer isn't looking to buy your job. And if you're a typical independent brick and mortar training gym (i.e. not a franchise), it's probably a stretch to think of your business as a true turnkey opportunity. Prospective buyers would need some interest in a part time operational role. This also makes it hard to pull off absentee ownership, which means you're looking for someone local. So your realistic pool of prospective buyers is vanishingly small.

All of this to say, while it's certainly possible to sell your gym, it's not likely you'll walk away with retirement money.

But take heart; if you run your business well, you can still have an amazing life doing what you love while creating great cash flow. And when properly utilized, this cash flow can fund all sorts of opportunities: buying the commercial property for your gym, tax-advantaged retirement plans, index investments, real estate investments, etc.

Sure, getting an enormous check would be a great way to end your time with your training gym. But even if that's not an option? A well-run business that creates strong net cash flow can still create a real financial future for you and your family.

BOCTAOE

Let's talk about my favorite acronym: BOCTAOE.

This is an important (and implicit) disclaimer to strong statements.

You see, when you write missives like I do, it can be annoying when every single statement is qualified with words like

"generally"

"usually"

"most of the time"

"in most circumstances"

etc. etc. etc.

But if we're being honest, virtually any statement you can make will have exceptions.

In other words...

BOCTAOE.

This is an acronym popularized by Scott Adams that stands for "but of course there are obvious exceptions."

You can tack this on to any strongly worded maxim because, well.... there are always obvious exceptions.

(I addressed this in the very first maxim in my 40 Years, 40 Lessons post about my personal life philosophies. It's my favorite piece I've ever written. You can find it on page 185).

In other words...

Training gym owners need to be making at least $175/avg. monthly revenue for large group class memberships.*

*BOCTAOE

To grow your training gym, you need some kind of low barrier offer so clients can try before they buy.*

*BOCTAOE

If you have more than three service offerings, your business will drown in complexity*

*BOCTAOE

Moral of the story: even the best business maxim is not correct in all situations. One of the key tasks of lifelong learners is the never ending process of contextualizing various pieces of business advice.

When faced with a maxim, rather than discount it if it doesn't fit your experience, ask yourself "under what circumstances would this be correct?"

Because if and when you think YOUR business is different, 99% of the time you're wrong.*

*BOCTAOE

What's The Best Business Book for Training Gym Owners?

What's the best business book for training gym owners?

The E-Myth Revisited by Michael E. Gerber.
If you haven't ever read it, go buy it right now and read it.

If you have read it, go read it again.

Currently during my yearly re-read, always a good use of my continuing education time.

Why Should You Start a Business?

Gentle reader, please indulge me as we're getting semi-philosophical.

There are lots of reasons to start a business.

To help more people.

To be the captain of your professional fate.

To have fun.

To increase your earning potential.

To learn and grow as a human being.

And these are all good reasons. And they all resonate with me. But there's a slightly loftier reason I think about a lot.

To test your philosophy of life.

This sounds out there (Burning Man guy over here, hi there, so great to meetcha!). But when you think about it, the list above are the desired *outcomes* of the business you build.

And your business is a machine; it's made of systems that are guided by a set of values, ideally pointed at a mission and en route to a vision, in service of a certain kind of human.

The systems are *what* you do.

The values are *how* you do it.

The mission is *why* you do it.

The vision is *where* you're going and *when* you'll get there.

And your client avatar is *who* you exist to serve.

As will shock exactly ZERO longtime readers, I think your personal values are the foundation. Yes, the mission matters, but your mission is a reflection of what your values are and what you believe to be important in life.

All the other pieces have to be a reflection of *what matters to you*. What you believe in your heart of hearts to be *true* about life, about how humans interact, and how to create win-win relationships.

You see, I think a small business is actually a chance to create "the city you want to live in." You get to test hypotheses of how humans can be with each other.

As any training gym owner knows, you're not a dictator. But you sure are the mayor.

Yes, you make the final call. But you're still beholden to your team and clients.

Because if you can't create a machine that builds order from chaos and balances the needs of all parties, these stakeholders will be displeased and will leave you. And a city is no fun when you're all alone. And if you're all alone, the game is over.

Or even WORSE, they stay. And you'll all be slightly unhappy together. Eek.

That's why I think all businesses are an opportunity to test a philosophy of life.

How should we treat each other as humans?

How do we fairly balance each other's needs when there's a zero sum conflict and you all can't get what you want?

How can we come together and seek to understand even when there's conflict?

How do we work together to make the best decision when each of us sees through a glass darkly?

What are the standards of behavior we can expect of each other?

How do we hold each other accountable when those standards are violated?

What's the best and fairest way to share the work and share the spoils?

How do we respond to adversity?

How do we manage the need for stability with the need for growth?

We strive to answer these questions by building a machine that reflects our very best answers.

And then we track data to keep score. The game of business gives you feedback about how satisfying your answers are to citizenship of your city.

PRO TIP: In spite of every disgruntled entrepreneur who's grumbled about his employees and clients, the issue is NOT your people. Therefore you can't solve your struggles by just getting new citizens. *Wherever you go, there you are.*

Some of the feedback is subjective. The comments you hear from your team, your clients, and not to be underestimated, *the feelings* you have about your business when you're lying awake in bed at night.

Some of the feedback is objective. The key performance indicators that tell you how you're doing: new trials sold, monthly revenues, terminations, profit margins, etc.

When taken together (and both matter), you'll be able to see how well your philosophy is working. And over time, you can refine your hypothesis.

Because unlike a sporting event, business is an *infinite game.*

Sometimes it makes sense to sell your business and start a whole new game. But the goal isn't to "win" and then be done.

The goal is to "keep playing."

And in the process of serving your community, becoming a more fully realized version of yourself.

I don't know about you, but I can't think of a better way to spend my days.

How Do I Know What to Work on in My Business?

One of the most common challenges we face as training gym owners is deciding what to work on next. After all, we have constraints of time, energy, and money.

And being a business owner can make you feel like you're snorting crushed up crazy pills, so it can be hard to think clearly sometimes.

Having a clear set of weekly or month metrics can help. All businesses need some kind of dashboard. These can quickly illuminate areas that are lagging and need more attention.

But you also have to consider the big picture.

Specifically, you have to **"begin with the end in mind"** and get clear on your vision for your dream business. Dashboards will tell you where you are, but they won't help you decide where you want to go.

That can only be answered with questions like:

- *What kind of business do you want?*
- *What kind of impact do you want to make on your community?*
- *What do you want your team and clients to be saying about their experience?*
- *What kind of work do you want to be doing?*
- *What kind of work do you NOT want to be doing?*
- *Who do you want to be working with?*
- *What kind of revenue do you want to make?*
- *What services are you offering?*
- *What are you legendary for?*

And these questions are beyond the scope of a KPI analysis. They require you to step outside of the day to day and get clear on what kind of future you're creating.

Here are a few best practices for creating a compelling vision for your business:

1) Get physically outside your business.

For most people, this kind of visioning work is best done somewhere besides your training gym. Since you're looking to think big and imagine a compelling future, you don't want to accidentally anchor yourself to the present.

I personally like to do this work in environments that inspire me, whether it be on vacation or a beautiful NYC hotel lobby. You may find you do your best dreaming while in nature. The key point is to break your daily patterns.

2) Create clarity on your personal goals.

Your business is not your life. But your business needs to work *with* your life. So it only makes sense to build your business vision AFTER getting clear on what you want for your personal life.

(For a done-for-you, 60 minute personal visioning process, head to businessforunicorns.com/book-stuff)

3) Write out a vision for your dream business on a specific date in the future.

There are a few different processes you can use for this. Cameron Herrold's *Vivid Vision* and Zingerman's ZingTrain Visioning Process are both worth exploring.

Although the exact time interval varies based on the process you use, you want it to be far enough away that you can dream big. I've always enjoyed Zingerman's 10ish year approach, but can see an argument for the slightly more accessible 3 year timeline.

Whatever timeline you choose, you're looking to create a detailed 2-5 page document that outlines every aspect of your future business. Be sure to include quantifiable targets (revenue, profit margin, number of clients and employees, etc.) AND qualitative targets (what do your clients and employees say about your business, how have you impacted your industry, how does it *feel* when you're in your training gym, etc.)

4) Use your vision to create your one year, quarterly, and weekly goals.

And now we arrive at the answer to our question: once you have your vision, work backwards to identify what you need to focus on NOW. Here's how...

First off, share your vision document with any other key stakeholders. Depending on the size of your training gym, this may only be one or two other key employees. But as soon as there are other team members with a meaningful role in bringing this vision to life, they need to be looped in. After all, no one can read your mind!

Then, review your document once every three months before your quarterly planning session.

(And if you're not already doing a quarterly planning session — like we facilitate in the Unicorn Society — that's something to add immediately.)

This clearly articulated vision will be used to create your one year goals. For instance, if you know you want to achieve X revenue in X year's time, this can inform where you want to be on that journey one year from now.

And in turn, these one year goals shape your focus for the next quarter. For this part of the process, it can be valuable to brain dump alllll the things you could potentially focus on in the next three months. Then methodically organize them with this question:

"Which of these goals, if achieved, will have the greatest positive impact on my business and move me closer to my dream business?"

By filtering your present challenges and opportunities through the lens of your long term vision, you'll be well situated to decide exactly what to focus on next with pigheaded discipline. And just as importantly, it will help you identify all the things you're NOT going to focus on for the next few months.

A final crucial point: "Plans never work, but planning always does."

While a compelling vision is a powerful tool, that's not because you'll (usually) create the exact vision. The value is in steering the ship and identifying where to focus next.

How Do I Get More Referrals?

Here's your move:

Instead of bribing clients to get you paying members, give your clients free stuff to give to their friends.

By all means, you should incentivize and reward your clients for spreading the word about your business. However, we have to appreciate that even the most ardent advocate of your biz would benefit from a very easy way for their friends to try you out.

Sure, you could direct them to your low barrier offer/trial. But if it's a traditional 14 to 30 day offer, and certainly if it's a *paid* offer, that still may be too high of a barrier.

A great workaround here is giving clients a free trial to give to their friends; this can even be positioned (correctly) as a VIP bonus. If you go this route, consider making this bonus offer time sensitive, so the friends in question have an incentive to take action or risk losing the perk.

While this can help, remember that prospects face more than simply financial costs; they have to spend time, energy, and the risk of feeling foolish. And a 14 to 30 day program — even if free — may still feel like a daunting mountain for a prospect who's uncertain if this will be the right fit.

That's why I've come to love "one or two free workouts." Admittedly, this adds another step to your funnel; you'll usually still want your prospects to move into the full LBO/trial experience, as a single class may not be enough for them to get fitness married to your training gym. It's also not the perfect fit for all training gym models.

But by making it easier to get started and lowering the commitment, your clients will have an easier time sharing the love with their pals.

When Your Heart Drops to Your Stomach: The Missing KPI

Sometimes you just gotta take a deep breath and do the scary thing.

Longtime followers of my fitness business musings know I repeatedly bludgeon you over the head with…

I mean…

Erm…

I consistently endorse the value of tracking key performance indicators (KPIs).

You can't measure everything that matters. But it's hard to manage anything that's not being measured.

That's why many KPIs are imperfect attempts at assigning numbers to qualitative domains.

As an example:

"On a scale of 1-10, how likely are you to refer our business to a friend?"

This question is at the heart of the Net Promoter Score system. At least in theory, it tracks how satisfied your clients are with your business. After all, this number identifies how likely people are to risk social capital recommending your business. This is a solid, if subjective, proxy for client satisfaction.

So let me offer a KPI as valuable for your personal life as your professional life:

How many difficult conversations are you currently avoiding?

1?

3?

7??

It's only natural; you're going to have feelings about stuff from time to time. This is inevitable when you care about something. And presumably, you care a LOT about your business.

Many times you'll be feelin' feelings about your team. And/or clients. And/or vendors. And/or anyone else in your business's orbit. Lots of these feelings are positive, which makes them easier to express. But sometimes those feelings trend a bit darker; hurt, upset, disappointed, angry, frustrated, etc.

The key is what you do about it.

Too often training gym owners — and humans — resist the difficult conversations required to move their business — and life — forward.

For instance, you know when you're feeling some kinda way about your team member because they've been repeatedly doing something that's frustrating you? When they walk in the gym, and you cordially say hi, but you're also pissed off they're only answering every third email?

Yep. That's what I'm talking about. That's your cue it's time to have a talk.

These chats aren't "fun." But when you become skillful and practiced, 95% of the time both parties feel much better on the other side.

You'll generally learn things you didn't know: including where you're invariably contributing to the problem. You'll understand the other person better and feel more closely connected. It will also free you of an emotional weight dragging your energy down.

Admittedly, this is trickier to pull off than I'm making it sound. But there are resources out there to learn this skill. Check out the books *Crucial Conversations* by Kerry Patterson, Joseph Grenny,

Ron McMillan and Al Switzler, and *Difficult Conversations* by Bruce Patton, Douglas Stone, and Sheila Heen.

You CAN learn to navigate these waters in an elegant and relationship-strengthening way.

And it's worth your time to invest in this skill.

Because the quality of your business (...and life!) is directly correlated to the number of challenging conversations you're willing to have.

NOTE 1: You're not under an obligation to have a chat every single time with every single person in your life.

Life is short. Your time and energy is finite. It's ok to intentionally decide you don't care enough about the individual. Emotionally successful humans know how to give themselves closure without requiring other parties to be involved. At its best, this is a form of healthy boundary setting.

Just be honest with yourself how often you play the "fuggit" card.

Because if you play the "fuggit" card with people that are truly important to you?

You're probably missing out on some gold.

NOTE 2: You will never succeed playing the "fuggit" card with your team.

If the situation is intractable and you've given up on a resolution, it's best to end the working relationship. To keep someone around when you've given up on them is inhumane.

The cave you fear to enter holds the treasure you seek.

How Do I Know What Advice To Follow?

If you read business books or follow "thought leader" types, you'll hear lots of persuasive arguments.

And many of these arguments contradict each other.

So it's important to put advice through this lens:

"Does this apply to <u>my</u> business at <u>this moment</u>?"

Even the best general advice is going to be incorrect when applied in the wrong context.

Alternatively, even a broken clock is correct twice a day.

This is why we need a filter. General advice can be helpful or harmful depending on when and how it's applied.

For instance, in the fitness business landscape, there are essentially two models for training gyms; a volume play with large group training, and a higher priced small group training model.

The former is the land of boutique fitness class franchises and bootcamps.

The latter is a more scalable version of personal training.

Both of these plays work. But the execution will be different: different low barrier offers, different pricing, different payout structures for staff, different complexities on how the service is delivered, different demands for equipment and physical facilities, etc. Each approach lends itself more or less naturally to different kinds of operators.

One of the most common missteps I see is a training gym owner applying a strategy for the wrong model and scratching their head as to why it's not working.

Furthermore, a strategy that works like gangbusters to take you from 40 to 60 clients won't always bear fruit when looking to go from 150 to 200 clients.

And keep in mind, this is only speaking to training gyms.

Many people who consume fitness business information are personal trainers growing their in-person biz or building an online brand. Yes, many principles overlap. But sound advice applied in an incorrect context will get poor results.

This isn't to say that one shouldn't look for strategies from other corners of the fitness industry. In fact, some of the best ideas come from other industries altogether.

It just means you have to ask:

"Does this apply to my business at this moment?"

How Do I Know When to Delegate?

Let's discuss the hands-down BEST pieces of advice... that's often poorly executed.

"Outsource, delegate, and hire people to do all tasks not in your Zone of Genius."

Overall, this advice is gold.

You should spend most of your time on the activities that drive the most value for your business. Invariably these are activities that are high impact, that you're world class at, and that give you energy.

This means all the boring, tedious, confusing, not-naturally-fun tasks and activities?

We want to get them off your plate.

As soon as you can, you want to outsource things like administrative work. You can find someone to do these tasks for a lower hourly rate than you could earn by doing higher value activities.

And most training gym owners will outsource some, most, or all of their training to a team that delivers your training systems.

But here's where you get into trouble: when you throw money at a missing skillset you don't understand.

The "Ugh-I-don't-wanna-think-about-it,-Here-you-just-do-it" approach leaves you at risk to bad actors. This happens for many training gym owners who hate marketing and sales and try to hire an agency to handle their lead generation.

This isn't to say you should never hire outside help. It makes sense to have someone else execute your plans and even collaborate on strategy.

But if you have no sense of the principles at play, how do you vet their work?

If you don't have reasonable benchmarks and targets, how will you know if you're getting the results you're paying for?

How will you compare that investment against the other ways you could invest that money?

It's appropriate to expand your capacity by delegating. And eventually, you'll want to hire people that are actually better and more skilled than you at a given role.

You don't need to (or want to) learn how to do everything yourself. I'm all for delegating.

But you at least need to understand *what success looks like.*

Otherwise you're not delegating, you're gambling.

What Are The Best Personal Finance Books for a Training Gym Owner?

Having a successful training gym means you receive an appropriate take-home income for your efforts. This includes a comfortable margin of profit after expenses.

But that's just the first part of creating long term financial well-being.

Once you're making a decent income, you've got to understand the basics of personal finance. Otherwise all those efforts won't pay off in the long run.

Personal finance can be daunting. This is in part because there's a whole industry incentivized to confuse you. Next, add in a dash of an emotionally fraught relationship with money. Now you've got a great recipe for throwing your hands up in the air.

By applying just a bit of effort to understanding the basics of personal finance, you can apply the 80/20 rule: focus on the 20 percent of your effort/activities that create 80 percent of your results.

To get started, read the following three books:

- *Automatic Millionaire* by David Bach
- *I Will Teach You To Be Rich* by Ramit Sethi
- *The Simple Path to Wealth* by J.L. Collins

You'll find much of the information overlaps. You'll review similar strategies approached from slightly different angles. And you'll build a solid base of knowledge to get your financial house in order.

The key thing will be to *take action.*

It's really not that complicated. But you do have to apply what you learn.

And money — like health and fitness — has a powerful emotional component that trips people up.

I'm not a financial professional. You'll get no specific advice from me on this topic. But this is NOT a topic where you can afford to stick your head in the sand.

I'm continually amazed how many very intelligent and successful people refuse to learn even the basics of investing because they don't want to think about it. This usually leads to hiring an advisor. Which sounds like they're smartly "outsourcing" to an expert.

But even a great advisor with very average fees can cut your retirement nest egg by up to 25%. :-/

Admittedly, as your investable assets grow, there's a time and a place to work with a professional.

But learn the basics first.

Or you'll have no way of knowing what help you're looking for. And this could cost you big.

What Are the Best Business Finance Books for Training Gym Owners?

To make money in your training gym, personal financial literacy is not enough. You need to have a basic understanding of *business finance*.

I know this isn't exactly the sexiest topic for most training gym owners. But you know what IS sexy?

Not being overdrawn on your bank account! To say nothing of making a solid income in exchange for your heart and hustle. :-)

Business finance for a typical training gym isn't that complicated. You don't need to have a fancy degree. But you DO need to understand the basics.

But what if you reeeeeally don't like this stuff?

The good news is that much of the day-to-day bookkeeping should be outsourced anyway.

And as to taxes? Paying for a qualified accountant is an investment that will almost always pay itself back with a solid return.

So a lot of the most unsavory bits will fall to others on your team.

But you DO need to have a solid grasp of the basics. You can outsource execution, but you'll still need to be able to understand what's happening with your business's finances.

If you need help on that front, read these books:

- *Profit First* by Mike Michalowicz
- *Profit First for Microgyms* by John Briggs
- *Simple Numbers* by Greg Crabtree
- *The Ultimate Blueprint for an Insanely Successful Small Business* by Keith J. Cunningham

I Changed My Mind [5 Topics]

Here are **five topics where I've changed my mind** over the past 11 plus years of running MFF.

Incentives

Inspired by books like *Drive*, I was originally committed to a world without financial incentives. Author Daniel Pink referenced studies where money hurt creativity and overweight the financial elements of the business. And who was I to argue with a bestselling author?

Based on this data, I felt the best path was to pay people fairly and trust their integrity to perform at a high level. I was concerned that performance based incentives would 1) be hard to track and 2) potentially create ugly second and third order consequences. While both of those concerns are valid, I no longer believe salary-only compensation for all non-owner roles does the trick.

For the best performance, most people — particularly ambitious high performers — need some financial skin in the game AND *deserve* some upside.

Scripts

For a long time I raged against any kind of scripts. I was worried it would constrain our team and make them feel stilted.

But in practice, any employee with a repeated interaction will say the same words the same way. For instance, you know that joke you *always* tell when consulting with a prospect? Yep, that's what I'm talking about.

The only question is whether those are the *best possible words* that consistently lead to the best outcomes.

Scripts don't have to suppress humanity. There's still a lot of room to be a human, to adjust rhythm and vocal inflection, and in rare cases, to throw the script out when truly appropriate.

But if you're not being consistent with verbiage in your most important conversations? You're relying on individual human judgement. And at least in theory, a script represents your team's *collective best thinking*. And that's better than a front line team member making it up as they go along.

Careers

When I opened up MFF, I sincerely thought it was possible for everyone that worked with us to open up their own Clubhouse. And I still think people with talent, hustle, and ambition can carve awesome paths within MFF.

The reality: for most training gyms, there are going to be natural limits to how fast the organization can grow. In most cases, there will also be a natural cap to how large the mature business will get. Furthermore, the skills required to be "intrapreneurial" are very specific; they need to have a proactive owner mindset, but not want to do their own thing.

I want MFFers to stay at MFF for as long as we're mutually happy with the arrangement. But for most training gyms and most employees, 2-5 years is the sweet spot before the individual needs to move on to keep growing and before the training gym needs fresh blood.

CAVEAT: This timeline seems to be on the longer side for less metropolitan markets, in part because there are less competing opportunities.

Marketing

Focusing on fulfillment and customer service alone will get you far if you're really, really good. And lord knows, we hit $4m in a single location without really understanding the basics of marketing. But if you want your business to have legs, at some point you have to learn the principles of marketing and sales to intentionally grow your business. Otherwise you're left hoping clients will refer friends. And hope isn't a strategy.

To be clear, a business can and should grow organically. If you're not getting referrals without having to ask, it means your service isn't good. And you can't fix poor fulfillment with strong acquisition.

To our defense, marketing isn't really a topic where we changed our mind per se. We always *knew* this was important. And we've always crushed "purple cow" branding. But it took us years to figure out how to create effective systems for growing the business.

NOTE: In my experience, most training gym owners are like young MFF. They *understand* this is important, but fail to realize how truly inadequate their skills are.

Metrics

This relates closely to the first topic. Part of the challenge with creating incentive plans is deciding what numbers to track with an individual's performance. For some roles — sales, for instance — this is simple. But for others, it's a bit trickier to settle on metrics that quantify performance.

More broadly, we knew there were subjective parts of the business that would benefit from data. But the tracking methods seemed both labor intensive and so imperfect as to be worthless (or so I thought).

For instance, utilization percentages for a given coach's session *could* be an indicator of how your clients feel about the coach. But we also know clients heavily weigh the time and day when choosing which sessions to attend. And there's no perfect way to scrub that confounder out.

But now I think this: imperfect tracking of subjective qualities is better than insisting on perfection and not tracking subjective qualities at all.

Not everything in your business can be easily quantified. But so long as you keep the inherent limitations in mind, "what gets measured gets managed."

Want help tracking KPIs and metrics? You can find a simple, non-intimidating overview at businessforunicorns.com/book-stuff.

Does Offering Discounts (Or Free Trials) Devalue Your Services?

No. Offering discounts or free trials does NOT devalue your services. In fact, they can be a powerful tool to grow your business.

But it's not always wise to hurt your revenues by reducing prices.

And if you're looking to create an incentive to inspire action by a certain deadline? It's often better to *add more value* with a time sensitive bonus offer or offers.

So how should we think about leveraging offers without hurting your business?

First off, discounted — or even free — trials are the best way to get lead flow. If you want any kind of scale in your business, you can't rely exclusively on pre-sold referred prospects who will sign up right away for a Core Offer with a one year commitment.

To put it another way, it's completely appropriate to give people a chance to "try before they buy."

It doesn't make you look cheap. Your actual monthly rates are still — or should be — premium as compared to other less valuable fitness solutions.

But by being generous upfront, you're acknowledging that you want to give this person an easy way to see if your services are a fit. As your business grows, this is all the more important. Because if you develop any marketing chops, you'll encounter a high percentage of people who find you without being pre-sold by other clients.

What about periodically offering promotions/discounts on your Core Offer(s)?

This can also serve its place BUT it can totally be overdone. The last thing you want to do is train your audience to wait for discounts. But used very judiciously, you can create compelling, time-sensitive, and quantity-limited offers to inspire people to take action.

This doesn't necessarily mean you always have to reduce prices. Perhaps you give your members a bonus pack of sessions or classes or a free nutrition consultation in exchange for signing up for a new membership by X date. Maybe you stack several bonuses together, including some discount on the first month.

Long story short, you can cut this cake a few different ways. But making compelling offers can give people the nudge they need.

Only word of caution: if you decide to use these kinds of offers, do NOT make a habit of wheeling-and-dealing. In other words, decide on the terms and don't waiver. If you do, you may condition clients to negotiate with you.

Your prices are not up for individual negotiation. You're just making a very specific time sensitive offer that people can take advantage of or not. Dassit.

Should You Bill Weekly or Monthly?

It's very rare that I speak in absolutes when it comes to success as a training gym owner.

But this is one of those moments.

I promise you, this is a move you need to make ASAP. After the logistical pain-in-the-butt-of-change is over, there's only massive upside.

Change your membership billing from monthly to weekly (or every 2 or 4 weeks).

(Cue laughter from our Australian training gym owners who've only ever done weekly billing.)

By moving to weekly billing you will:

- Improve conversion by making the price point feel smaller at point of sale
- Improve your cashflow with a steady drip of cash
- Increase total yearly revenue with a "13th month"
- Solve the 5 Mondays problem (where clients pay for sessions or classes in multiples of 4 that leave left over days in months with 30 or 31 days)
- Match weekly or bi-weekly payroll with revenue
- Make future price increases feel smaller
- Catch declined credit cards faster

Now, in the spirit of turning over the rock from all the angles, you *could* point to these items as downsides of weekly billing:

- You may see a modest increase in the amount of declined credit card chasing
- Most merchant services charge a (super) small fee per transaction, so you'll pay slightly more in transaction fees
- Some clients won't like it if they're used to paying bills monthly.

At MFF, we quote the weekly price, but bill every four weeks. This allows us to get most of the benefits (minus steadier drips of cash) while mitigating the first of the two downsides.

It also allows us to give clients four weeks to use their allotment of credits. So if they sign up for a 2x per week membership, they get 8 credits each time their card is billed.

Admittedly, the "every 4 weeks" approach can lead to more confusion for some clients who may now have a harder time tracking their billing date. But the advantages massively outweigh the disadvantages.

The biggest barrier for most training gym owners is that it's a lot of work to change your billing. But on the other side is a better business.

Simple Marketing Calendar for a Training Gym [Easy]

If you're not already using one, creating a marketing calendar is one of the single most important tools for planning and executing a well thought out marketing plan. By putting some thought into what offers you'll make at what time of year, you'll never be caught scrambling to execute a seasonal time sensitive promotion.

Here's a SUPER simple way to tackle it without making it overly complicated…

1. Open up a document (or if you prefer a spreadsheet) on your computer and create a heading for each month.
2. For each month, identify the opportunity for messaging: holiday, season, anniversary, etc. For example, November is Black Friday/Cyber Monday, December is the holidays. January is the New Year, etc. etc.
3. For each month, draft out 1-3 messages or special promotions broken down by segment (Current Clients, Former Clients, Unconverted Prospects).

For instance, January is always a big time of year for fitness. Perhaps you do a flash sale of your low barrier offer for Unconverted Prospects ("Get our trial for $9 instead of $99"), and a targeted "we want you back" promotion for Former Clients.

Maybe you decide to use February to offer a special limited-time-only offer to save money with a year paid-in-full. ("Let's celebrate Valentine's Day by getting fitness married for the year!") You can offer this to Current Clients as an upgrade and to Former Clients and Unconverted Prospects as a new agreement. Maybe you even toss in another value-add bonus like a free nutrition consultation.

March is often a tough time of year for people to stay motivated. So maybe you charge a modest fee to run an accountability challenge for your Current Clients where they can compete for prizes. You can keep promoting your ever-green low barrier offer to Unconverted Prospects via your usual marketing channels, but put your focus on the experience of your Current Clients for this month.

Once we're into April, spring feels close. This could be an opportunity to run a "Swing into Spring" offer of some kind.

Etc. etc. etc.

In my experience, most training gym owners understand the value of this kind of planning. But it can feel unwieldy and daunting. And because there are so many day-to-day demands, too often this kind of planning takes a back seat.

Complexity is the enemy of execution. Keep it simple.

You can build out the bones of a simple marketing calendar with a strong cup of coffee and a dedicated hour of work.

It doesn't need to be perfect, just get it done.

Then use your calendar to prepare any needed materials (emails, ads, landing pages, physical signage, digital ads, social posts, etc.) one to two months in advance.

Voila! Marketing calendar greatness is yours.

36 Hours of Pain

One of the hardest parts of running a business is "ripping off band-aids."

The band-aid in question can be any number of situations demanding a change:

- A pricing model that won't allow for profitability
- A long term employee that's no longer working out
- A new hire that didn't turn out to be the right fit
- A service offering that's not as good as other options
- A scheduling or billing software that's clunky
- An ad agency that's not delivering the promised results
- A lease that's too onerous for your business to thrive

I could go on and on, but you get the point.

Now let's consider the two barriers to making the change:

1) You're not 100% sure that your proposed alternative will really be better.

Sometimes the grass just *looks* greener. Indeed, this is a sticky widget and will require some careful thinking on your part.

While careful thinking is required to make this assessment, for now let's focus on barrier #2.

2) All change meets with resistance.

This often comes in the form of emotional pushback from those involved. This is especially so if they believe they will be negatively impacted.

Sometimes that's a clear cut concern: if you're letting someone go, this is usually not their preferred play.

Sometimes the changes may be for the long term good of all parties, but you'll *still* get resistance.

Any meaningful change will involve logistical hurdles. And even if YOU are confident the change will make everyone's lives better over the long term, most humans don't like change. Particularly if you're making a decision they disagree with in good faith.

But you'll still need to get over the hump.

If you believe in your heart of hearts that ripping off a band-aid will facilitate the best possible version of your business... then you have to do the hard thing.

Your role is to serve the extended community.

This means balancing the needs of your clients, your employees, and the shareholders as best you know how. And occasionally, this will require creating discomfort for some parties; not the least of which is you!

This has been one of the hardest lessons I've had to learn. If you care deeply about people's feelings, it can be hard to do things that will result in people being upset with you.

So let me offer a phrase that comes from the book *Traction* and its Entrepreneurial Operating System:

"36 hours of pain."

When you find yourself agonizing about firing an employee, or raising your prices, or any other necessary change, it's going to hurt like hell for 36 hours.

And then it will be done.

To be clear, this isn't to say you should make changes willy nilly. You still need to make sure the appropriate people weigh in as you decide how to proceed.

You still need to communicate WHY the change is happening and roll it out well.

You still need to have individual conversations, help people process the change, and even let them vent when necessary.

But when you know the right call and you're hemming and hawing…

Remember you've got a mere 36 hours of pain ahead of you.

And on the other side is a better business for you, your clients, and your employees.

15 Traits of Successful Training Gym Owners

I've been reflecting on the differences between training gym owners who just get by and *those who thrive*.

Listen, this can be a tough biz. And we can't totally discount luck.

However, we should focus on what we CAN control.

Here's my observations about what sets the "Super-Achiever" training gym owners apart.

- They're genuinely excellent at the services they offer. This doesn't necessarily mean the finer points of program design and technical coaching (though it can, and ideally does). But at the very least, great training gym owners create an awesome training experience.

- They understand and empathize with what a typical client actually wants. Their focus is not on their own particular interests in training, methodologies, tools, status with other coaches, etc.

- They take the time to regularly fill their cup *physiologically*. This includes: taking time away from the business to rest, working out consistently, eating well, getting regular sleep, etc. In other words, doing what they advise their clients. :-)

- They take the time to regularly fill their cup *psychologically*. This includes: reflecting on how their work expresses meaningful personal values, connecting with loved ones, creating a compelling vision of their future, etc.

- They're as interested in business as they are in training and program design.

- They're as interested (or more!) in their clients as in they are in training and program design.

- They do not fear money. They understand their business

finances, their personal finances, and they have clearly articulated financial goals for both.

- They devote time, money, and energy to education via conferences, books, courses, coaching, etc.
- They're willing to be honest and vulnerable about where they and their business may be struggling.
- They work on unaddressed emotional blocks that get in their way via self-work modalities like therapy, coaching, journaling, plant medicine, etc.
- They have high standards. They consistently keep their commitments, which brings them high self-esteem and a belief in their own self-efficacy.
- They have a bias for action balanced against the ability to periodically slow down and reflect on next steps.
- They're not afraid of success. They know change is required for growth. This will, at times, bring criticism and judgment from family, friends, employees, and loyal long term clients who have reasons for wanting them to stay the way they are; they accept this fact.
- They value excellence, even when it means making the hard changes to their business needs.
- They know the very skills and attributes that brought them praise and any success they've had so far may be the very attributes preventing them from getting to the next level.

3 Contexts for Entrepreneurial Success

I want to share a powerful framework that encapsulates why I'm so passionate about the Unicorn Society and being a part of a like-minded community that shares your goals and values.

But first, lemme tell you a quick story.

Your ol' pal Mark had some ups and downs during the early stages of the ol' pandemic.

I suspect I'm not alone. Maybe you can relate.

When I look back at this rollercoaster, there's obviously some correlation between challenging circumstances and my mindset.

And that makes sense; when the whole world seems like a dumpster fire and your business is getting throttled, it can be hard to stay plucky.

Even for me. And to the dismay of people revolted by enthusiasm, I am *pathologically plucky.*

But you know what correlates even MORE tightly with my mental well-being?

My context.

Specifically, three kinds:

- My attentional/intellectual context
- My environmental/physical context
- My social context

1) Attentional/Intellectual Context

As the saying goes, "garbage in, garbage out."

Are you reading books, podcasts, and EMAILS FROM YOUR FRIEND MARK that lift you up?

Or are you compulsively scrolling through Instagram or the news?

I'm not advocating you tuning out the world at large. I am saying you will be more effective at impacting that world when you're intentional about where you're placing attention. Specifically, monitor the type, source, and volume of media you're consuming.

2) Environmental/Physical Context

Outside of choosing where to live — both your home and geographic location — this one isn't all that easy to change.

However, the physical environments where you spend time have a massive impact on you. If your office or training gym are not clean and organized and inspiring, this is something worth addressing.

For many people, including your author, this is why travel is so powerful. Getting out of our usual routines and being exposed to different places can shake us out of ruts. It can challenge us to think differently and open up our minds. And if you're someone that *loves* to travel, it will also give you energy and inspiration.

3) Social Context

It's painfully cliché, but nonetheless true. You are massively impacted by the people you spend time with.

Your choice of friends, professional networks, and official and virtual mentors creates your personal reference group. And we are compelled by evolutionary wiring to adopt the mindsets, behaviors, and values of the social waters we swim in.

So once again, being intentional about your community will massively influence your mental well-being (or lack thereof).

****

And THIS is why I'm on fire about the value of professional networking groups like the Unicorn Society; good ones will hit all three buckets.

They provide good inputs for your **attention/intellectual** context.

They provide an opportunity to get out of your day-to-day and experience rejuvenating and novel **environmental/physical** contexts.

And they give you a powerful community and growth-minded **social** context.

A final note...

Being in a better place mentally will also lead to more material success. And that's all well and good.

But here's the thing: any achievement or material success is just one path to a good headspace.

The real goal is the mental well-being that comes from being of service.

By engaging in meaningful work and connecting deeply with other humans.

The tools above can help your business's prospects.

But they also cut out the middleman and bring you directly to improved mental well-being.

And then?

You'll be more likely to make good decisions that move your professional ball forward anyway.

(Hat tip to Darren Hardy's book *The Compound Effect* that inspired this framing.)

The Process Is the Point

Ultimately, your business is not actually about "getting it done."

It's not really about the destination.

It's a dance; it's a song.

Is there something currently presenting a major issue in your business?

Have you noticed that there's pretty much ALWAYS something presenting an issue in your business?

Your journey HAS to have ebbs and flows and challenges and adventures. That's what makes it valuable. Otherwise the whole thing would be boring.

And we want a game worth playing.

And while it's normal to be stressed sometimes, a game worth playing is best played with joy and curiosity and excitement.

Because really, it's about *who you become* along the journey.

How Can I Sell Without Feeling Sleazy?

First point: if you're concerned about this, you probably don't need to worry.

As a rule, training gym owners concerned about turning people off or being too pushy usually don't need to be overly concerned. In fact, when this is a worry, it suggests you may be *too* passive in your approach.

When you structure a client-centered sales conversation, the goal is to get on your client's agenda and be as helpful as possible.

You help your client clearly identify what they want, and when appropriate, offer them a solution. That's not pushy. It's actually good customer service! In fact, when you think about it that way, it would be weird NOT to make them an offer.

Here are the four key pillars of this kind of conversation.

1) Build rapport and set expectations for the convo.

When you start your chat, do some icebreaking.

You don't need to spend thirty minutes connecting over a shared hobby, or asking endless questions about their kids. On the other hand, it's a wee bit weird if you launch into Step 2 without at least checking in about how their day's going.

Additionally, at some point during the beginning of the chat, you want to share (or reiterate) expectations:

- You're going to spend about X many minutes together
- You'll ask some questions to make sure you're clear on their goals
- You'll share a bit about how your gym works
- Finally, if you think it could be a fit, you'll offer some ways to work together.

2) Identify their most important goals, why they matter, and

previous obstacles.

During this part of the chat, you want to ask some specific questions so that you — and the prospect — are absolutely clear on their goals.

Ex. If you had a magic wand, what changes would you make to your health and fitness?

You then follow up to peel the onion so you — and the prospect — are absolutely clear on WHY that goal matters to them.

Ex. Can you say a bit about why that's important to you?

Finally, you'll also want to identify any obstacles they may need support with.

Ex. What's gotten in the way of you achieving these goals in the past?

For bonus points, you can gather some intel on their logistics: how many times they can work out per week, their monthly budget, their preference between individual, small group, or larger group coaching, etc.

3) Build value for your services by showing how your training gym will help them achieve *their* goals and solve *their* obstacles.

This section will look different based on your model.

It could be an assessment of some kind, a mini-workout, a full-on workout, a tour, or just a presentation about your business.

The key thing here is to focus on the *benefits* that the components of your training gym offer.

In other words: *A lot of our members struggled with getting bored before working with us. That's why we [fill in the blank with how you address this] to make sure you stay engaged.*

Two more pro tips:

- No one cares about the features. A tour of your equipment doesn't matter. Your client cares about *their* goals, not *your* process. And certainly not your cool set of battle ropes. It's ok to share the features. But you have to link it back to how it will achieve *their* goals and solve *their* obstacles.

- You don't need to tell them every single thing. Focus only on the features that relate to *their* goals and solving *their* obstacles. Don't sell them on your solutions for problems they don't have.

4) Make an ask with a compelling offer

Finally, after gathering all their data and building value for your services, it's time to make the ask.

The key here is to *make an explicit membership recommendation* that works for their logistics and is the best fit for their goals.

For bonus points, consider using some kind of highly attractive and irresistible time sensitive offer as an incentive for signing up today.

Then wait in silence.

For as long as it takes.

Then get your new client signed up. :-)

****

To state the obvious, this is about as high level as you get. The art and science of sales includes a LOT more than this simple framework: pre-framing the conversation, getting in the right state before the call, testing different questions, exploring different ways to build value, pricing strategy, addressing objections, etc. etc. etc.

However, by comparing the above framework against your script (YOU DO HAVE A WRITTEN OUT SCRIPT RIGHT?), you'll get some ideas to make your sales conversations 1% better, *without* feeling sleazy or pushy.

"Don't Drive Angry"

If you run a business, I bet that sometimes you have *feelings*.

This is normal. It means you care!

And feelings are helpful signals. We don't want to dismiss them or attempt to repress them. That never works anyway. We want to acknowledge them, feel them in our body, and process them in constructive ways. This usually happens via conversation with a caring human.

On the other hand, when you're super duper pissed off, it's usually not the bestest time to make a big decision about your business.

This can be particularly tough if you have a strong bias for action. When you're confronted by a challenging situation, you may feel a strong pull to solve it NOW, or if possible, YESTERDAY.

But when you're feeling heated, it's best to slow down. Before you dash off that email response, consider the coaching of one of my mentors, Ari Weinzweig of Zingerman's Deli:

When you get furious, get curious.

Again, we're not trying to be Spock. When you care deeply about something, it's only normal to feel some feelz at times.

While you can't always control your emotional response, you can — at least in theory — prevent yourself from taking action right away.

This kind of impulse control isn't easy.

But I can't think of a single time that a big decision about a heated topic didn't benefit from sleeping on it and circling back to it the next morning.

Ommmmm.

5 Lessons from 2021

After making it through the pandemic, 2021 was particularly fertile for growth.

Every year, I take some time at year end to recap what learnings I will be taking forward. While I can't do justice to all the lessons learned, here are a few things that were on my mind as I looked forward to 2022.

**** Originally written in December 2021 ****

Dial in your hiring process.

Over the course of the last year, MFF turned over our entire business team. Literally.

Our most tenured non-trainer staff member started full time in December of 2020(!).

While we've had lots of amazing people over the years, I'm absolutely on fire about our current team. Part of this is because every time we've made a hire we look to improve our process. Each at bat gives us a chance to get even clearer on 1) exactly what we're looking for and 2) exactly what new hires can expect at MFF.

We've had the opportunity to do a lot of hiring this year. These extra "reps" tightened up an already-pretty-strong process for hiring new MFFers. We've made several small but meaningful improvements to the hiring SOP. In an era where labor shortages seem to bedevil many businesses, for whatever reason, we haven't struggled to find awesome candidates.

If I HAD to guess, I'd attribute some of our success on this front to our colorful, quirky brand. One look at MFF's website attracts the right kind of candidate, and importantly, sends everyone else running away screaming. ;-)

If you don't have a written down repeatable process that you use *every single time* you make a hire, get thee to your SOPs and make it so. This is even MORE important if you don't make hires all that often.

Your success is your people. Period. The better you get at screening and hiring, the more successful you'll be. And frankly, the more fun you'll have.

Use Virtual Assistants to increase your capacity.

I realize not every training gym has enough overflow of tasks to justify using VAs. However, if you're finding that you or your team are spending lots of time on repetitive tasks that don't require higher level critical thinking, this could be an awesome solution to create more capacity.

If you're looking for a solution, we've had great success with VAs for Gyms.

VAs for Gyms has freed up hours of time for our team. We spend less time pulling reports, processing registrations, updating landing pages, or doing any number of outsourceable tasks. This means we can spend more energy and effort on high touch customer service and driving the business forward.

Even better, since we work with an agency that specializes in gyms, they come preloaded with a number of helpful SOPs. Plus, since it's an agency, they handle the management of their staff of VAs and maintain a team of VAs with different expertises for different tasks.

Worth a look! Learn more at vasforgyms.com

Disclosure: If you check out VAs for Gyms and tell 'em I sent you, BFU gets a small commission. Regardless of whether you mention BFU or not, it's a service that's been very valuable for us.

Find "same-but-different" educational resources.

My educational growth and speed has been super-charged in

2021. I attribute this to going back to the basics. Or, to put a slightly more fine point on it, finding some "same-but-different" educational resources that were brand new to me.

In other words, I took up a serious study of adjacent types of fitness businesses: most notably fitness franchises and the enormous number of current or former Crossfit gyms usually referred to as microgyms. Related, as I expanded my lens, I found a handful of new fitness business gurus that speak to these specific corners of the biz.

This is a bit different from past years. Historically, my focus has been on:

1) Training gyms just like MFF and a known pantheon of fitness business experts who speak to this model.

2) Broader business training, courses, and books from nationally known "thought leaders" in other industries.

Both of those buckets are still valuable.

But by leveraging podcasts, hiring coaches, getting back to attending events (and not only as a speaker!), and looking into investment opportunities in franchising, I've learned a TON. These new skills and contacts will benefit MFF and our BFU clients in the years to come.

Related, here's a quote from child psychologist Dr. Becky that blew my head open and is officially a new mantra:

"Don't label me an "expert;" it's an anti-learning term."

CAROL DWECK GROWTH MINDSET IN DA HIZ-OUSE.

Know your numbers. Really. SERIOUSLY.

Stick with me, as I know you've heard this from me before...

This year saw yet another quantum leap in my studies of business finance. This is a topic I've felt relatively ok on for the past few years. But as we transitioned into a new (external) bookkeeping team, I've become much more engaged with all of MFF's numbers on a monthly, weekly, and even daily basis.

In 2020, I studied and learned every set of suggested benchmarks I could get my hands on, both inside our industry, and for small service businesses at large.

In 2021, I came to *really* understand what that meant for MFF.

On the micro, this allowed us to create even better dashboards with even clearer optics for what's going on in our business. With better real-time weekly data, we can make better decisions about how to allocate resources.

On the macro, I beefed up my understanding of the Balance Sheet and Cash Flow Statements. Profit and Loss statements will tell you a lot of what you need to know in a modest service business without inventory. But even at MFF, I had some double-forehead-slap surprises hit me this year because I wasn't paying careful attention to all three financial statements.

Furthermore, as I've studied various franchise models in various industries, I now have a deeper understanding of the way the numbers look in all kinds of businesses.

In addition to the value for MFF, this context adds another layer of analysis and guidance for Unicorn Society members as we help them steer their ship.

Allow me to refer you to businessforunicorns.com/book-stuff to get your hot little hands on a simple overview for understanding and implementing KPIs.

You don't have to live your life like you're on probation.

"When will you stop living your life like you're here on probation?"

So what does this mean for intrepid, ambitious training gym

owners?

Well, that depends on what you need to hear.

But if you — like your pal Mark — sometimes get caught up in the hamster wheel…

If you sometimes tie your entire value as a human to what you DO…

Perhaps you can make some space to BE.

Maybe you can continue working on your business like a happy craftsperson, AND trust that your presence at the Grand Dance is enough.

We're all happy to see you here.

You belong.

What Kind of Help Do You Need?

A simple question: *What kind of help do you need?*

You see, sometimes, we know the root of a given issue and we know how to solve it. We just haven't made it a priority to fix it. Fixing this may require some accountability and a kick-in-the-ass, but we at least know what the issue is.

Other times, we know the issue, but aren't sure how to solve it. This is where a one-off call with a consultant or studying best practices can be helpful.

Still other times, we face the thorniest knot: we know we're not getting the results we want, but we're not exactly sure what the issue is.

And the worst case scenario?

When you THINK you know the root of your issue… but you're wrong.

This means spending time, energy, and money working for a fix without seeing traction. Because you're not actually solving the root of the issue.

Eek.

At the very least, you can start moving towards some progress by identifying *the number one* current issue in your business.

In other words:

If you had a magic wand and could change *one thing* about your business, what would you change and how would it be different?

This question should inform setting your quarterly goals. It also needs to be asked on a daily basis.

Until you know your most important priority, it's hard to solve it. Because even if you hire a coach, you can't articulate the kind of help you need.

Happily, we have a really cool resource that can help.

Head to businessforunicorns.com/book-stuff and check out our Training Gym Owner's Report Card.

It will help you identify where your business needs help, which will point you in the right direction.

Does Your Facility Look Like SH*T?

Maybe that's the issue.

Now I don't actually know, of course. I probably haven't been to your facility.

But some fitness facilities do look like doodoo.

As the oft-quoted, possibly made-up, but still reasonable-to-believe stat goes, the number one reason people leave gyms is due to **lack of cleanliness**.

And of course, if you hope to offer a premium product, having a clean space is really just the first step. To the extent that your budget allows, premium clients want to work out in a premium space.

This means more than mere cleanliness. It means good design features that reflect your brand. Your space should look *and feel* like a place your ideal client avatar wants to spend time in.

The lion's share of training gym owners lack a true passion — or aptitude — for design. While you don't need to be featured in *Architectural Digest*, you do want a minimally acceptable level of aesthetics. And that means you may need to look for some help.

(And no, you can't use Keeler, I already got him. Though if you're in **the Unicorn Society** and need help, you kind of got him *too.* I think getting Keeler's design skills on your space would be the ultimate-super-wowza-Ninja-use of his skills. So maybe DO use Keeler for a coaching call to get his two cents. Find out more at businessforunicorns.com.)

I also want to acknowledge MFF runs a 1) relatively high volume space 2) in NYC. We're always looking to make the space cleaner, prettier, and better. But those two facts make this hard, time consuming, and expensive.

Your space may not see quite the same wear and tear in other (cleaner) markets with less traffic. But regardless, you'll pretty much always need to be re-investing in your space.

Tossing out dirty, fraying bands, foam rollers, and Airex pads.

Repainting walls.

Spicing up the design.

Replacing furniture.

Changing out or upgrading equipment.

Etc. etc. etc.

These things matter, not only for their function. Because if your space seems uncared for, you're sending the wrong message to your clients.

Rather than being endlessly surprised that something always needs a refresh, best to accept that this process doesn't end.

PRO TIP: Consider making a monthly deposit to a dedicated bank account devoted exclusively to space upgrades.

File this whole topic under "Things you didn't realize you'd need to spend lots of energy on when you opened up a training gym."

But just like the other items in there, you can absolutely get the results you need with a bit of effort.

"How Much Do You Make?" [Net Owner Benefit]

How much do you make running your training gym?

A simple question.

For most people, the answer doesn't require much thought.

But it can be a bit tricky to answer for an entrepreneur.

Is that how much is on your tax return?

Not really. Your tax return is a *tax treatment*. Most lifestyle entrepreneurs have certain expenses — like your cellphone, for instance — covered by the business. This means it's a business expense. It won't show up as income on your return, even though you benefit from it.

Ok. What about the profit on your Profit & Loss Statement?

Samesie. That same cellphone will reduce your "profit." Furthermore, if you invest in big stuff, it won't show up as an expense on your profit and loss statement, at least not all at once. This means you may show a "profit" without necessarily having access to the cash.

What you're really looking for is something called "Net Owner Benefit."

The Net Owner Benefit of your business is exactly what it sounds like: the total (financial) benefit you get as a business owner.

This includes your actual-cash-in-bank income. We can break this bucket down between any salary you take, and any profit distributions/draws you take.

But importantly, Net Owner Benefit also includes legitimate business expenses — like your cellphone, computer, office supplies, etc. — that you need for the business to function, but also have personal benefit to you. It also includes benefits you receive as an employee, like health insurance or a 401k match.

For a typical training gym owner, this bucket can really add up. Since your business can purchase these items with pre-tax money, the savings can really add up.

Lastly, you have a category of business expenses that author Keith Cunningham colorfully calls “Owner Hoo-Haw”: a hilarious term for the lifestyle expenses you (legally) put on the business, but that you maaaaay not authorize for an operator you hired to replace you.

Examples: your car payments, staying an extra day for an educational event instead of red-eyeing back, hiring your children (!), exorbitant professional education budget, renting your home to your business to throw an event, etc. etc. etc.

These items may or may not make sense from a cash flow perspective. And these Owner Hoo-Haw items may or may not actually move your business forward. But it’s certainly another bucket of potential benefit for a business owner.

So when considering how much you “make,” a clear-eyed assessment would include all of the above categories. If you’re not already tracking these items, it could be worth considering. This is the only way to really understand how well you’re doing: as a percentage of revenue and from year-to-year.

Pro Tip: Perks are a bit trickier to track, but you can set up your P&L reports to make this easier. At the very least, track your net bank deposits on a monthly and yearly basis.

Money’s not all that matters. But it’s hard to help people if you’re broke.

The Requirement

I'm not one for dogmatism.

But some principles are essentially laws of nature.

And if you're looking to run a successful training gym?

Success requires investment.

This is true no matter how you define "success."

Want to make a bigger impact with your business?

Want to be a better partner to your spouse?

Want to improve your bloodwork?

Want to be ready to retire when the time comes?

Then you've got to invest: time and/or money and/or energy. For big results, usually all three.

If you don't make the commitment, you don't get the result.

This is true for our clients. And it's true for us as owners.

This investment doesn't necessarily need to be financial. But none can deny, big financial investments are a "forcing function." This carries much of the freight in keeping you accountable to take action.

In the past few months, I signed up for (yet another) very expensive coaching group and a very expensive fitness coach.

Part of what I'm paying for is their guidance and coaching.

But it's also a way to burn the boats; it's a forcing function. Because the money is now committed. So it's up to me to devote the time and energy to the resources provided so I can create the desired outcomes.

CONFESSION: On some level, this fact annoys me. Because I know it's the type of self-serving psychological rationale that salespeople use to justify charging exorbitant prices for services and products that don't necessarily have intrinsic value.

But I have to admit. I've come to reluctantly accept this as a fact of life.

Admittedly, I'm still not a fan of "Just put it on your credit card… or better yet, put a lien on your house!… it's like, you know, *The Secret!!* … what the mind can achieve!!!!!!…"

BUT

You get out of anything what you put into it.

I do think this can be taken to an unhelpful extreme. But there's no doubt that having skin in the game matters.

Think about it; have you ever tried to give away your services for free?

How much compliance did you get?

My point exactly.

Skin-in-the-game matters.

Boundaries [Tales of MF as a Bad Waiter :-/]

A while back, one of our Unicorn Society members shared this insightful thought in a post:

"I thought I was running a *people first* business. But now I realize it's been a *people pleaser* business."

Ouch!

Let's look at the difference between being "people first" vs being a "people pleaser."

And let's do so through the lens of a young Mark Fisher serving lasagna and wine at a fancy, high-end NYC Italian restaurant.

Your author's skills as a waiter, such as they are, can be accurately described as *severely limited*.

At this point in my life, I didn't have much experience eating out in *any* restaurants, let alone fancy(ish) ones. I'm from a family of six kids. So "going out to eat" in the Fisher household generally consisted of hitting up Mickey D's.

I didn't even find out about the whole "put your napkin in your lap" thing till I was in college while visiting my girlfriend's family.

And when I DID go out to eat, you can be sure my ass would mainly scan the prices to look for the cheapest thing on the menu. Because young aspiring actor in NYC with no trust fund and/or parental financial support.

So when I got hired to wait tables, I was not primed for success. I *wanted* to do a good job. But I wasn't really able to appreciate what the restaurant was attempting to sell.

But at the very least, I DID want to have positive experiences with the humans I worked with.

Alas, this was not a culture that made this goal terribly easy.

You see, in the high-stakes, hyper-competitive world of NYC hospitality, our management was used to handling demanding rich people. And there seemed to be an informal system:

The worse the customer treats us and our staff, the better treatment and more free stuff they get.

(Let me acknowledge my bias: this was a long time ago. I'm certain I wasn't totally fair or generous in how I viewed our management. Nonetheless, this was indeed my — and the staff's — general sense of how things played out.)

This approach created a perverse system of incentives.

The more horribly a customer treated the staff, the more they got. This meant these individuals were MORE likely to become repeat customers.

It was as if the restaurant *trained* the customers to treat us all like shit.

So what does this have to do with your training gym?

It's this:

You have to balance generosity, kindness, and a service mindset with clear and consistent boundaries.

This is one of THE hardest razor edges to find in any service business.

On the one hand, if you're easily aggrieved and you assume your customers are always trying to take advantage of you, you're going to struggle. After all, none of us are perfect every day. Oftentimes customers get upset with your business in proportion to the height of their expectations. So dismissing any brusque customer as an asshole and sending them on their way isn't exactly living up to the spiritual calling of world-class customer service.

On the other hand, if we have NO boundaries…

If there is virtually NOTHING a customer can do to get fired…

If you have clients that consistently disregard your policies, ask for exceptions, and somehow "forget" the same terms of their agreement over and over and over again…

You've got an issue on your hands.

Not only that, but if your team feels they have to put up with abusive behaviors, you'll lose credibility as a leader. I'm pained to admit it, but in my desire to relentlessly pursue "unconditional positive regard," this has absolutely happened in my career.

Perhaps one of the biggest personal shifts I've made as a business owner — and human — is curating the conviction to set and enforce boundaries. It's taken years of effort. And plenty of therapy. And I'm STILL not 100% cured of my "people pleaser" tendencies. But I am better than I've ever been.

SIDE NOTE: This is an example of how your personal quirks and wounds will directly impact your business unless you're willing to walk on the fire coals and address them head-on.

I speak from personal experience when I say it's VERY hard to find this line.

Personally, I will always choose naïveté over paranoia when it comes to client intentions. I believe we should start by being generous: give the benefit of the doubt, express sincere care and concern when dealing with an upset client, and always look for how we're contributing to a given miscommunication.

However…

If your business does any kind of volume, a certain percentage of your clients will be culture-killers. They will only be able to see things from their side, and they will want as much as possible, and they will genuinely freak out anytime they don't get their way. That's not being cynical. That's just math.

Now I'm NOT saying: "Armor up!" We don't want to answer customer service emails ready for a fight.

But we also have to rigorously track when we make exceptions so we can appropriately handle repeat offenders.

We can be charitable and kind AND sometimes fire clients.

And even when we have to (rarely) take this extreme action, we can still believe they're doing the best they can from where they are and want the best for them.

We don't have to fall into the trap of making them a "villain." We don't have to make ourselves a "victim." We don't have to deny them the fullness of their humanity.

But we can be adults.

We can set boundaries and end a relationship that isn't working for both parties.

Because we're dealing with some values-based decision-making, I don't have a formula for you on this topic.

But here's a crude framework:

1) You should rarely — if ever — boot a client for a single difficult encounter. We all have our moments, and you never know what's going on in a client's life. The obvious exception is if a client threatens your staff or other clients' safety.

2) You should track both policy exceptions and difficult experiences in your CRM so you can find patterns.

3) Once a client has stepped into the land of repeat offenders, at the very least, have a conversation with them about the pattern you're seeing. Since you have careful records, you can point to specific behaviors and make clear asks for how you'd like to see the relationship change.

4) For the sake of your business, your other clients, your team, and your own well-being, there has to be a boundary past which you're willing to end the relationship. It shouldn't happen often. And in most cases, outside of something truly egregious like threatening your staff's safety, only after you've had at least one direct conversation.

Running a business is not for the faint of heart.

But you can't polish a diamond without pressure.

The Time I Felt Lowest About Myself (And MFF)

Humans are funny creatures.

I've recently found myself digging into the rabbit hole of "Mimetic theory" and the work of philosopher Rene Girard.

Girard was a professor at Stanford and was a big influence on a few Silicon Valley luminaries. I was vaguely familiar with his work, but after reading Luke Burgis's (excellent) book *Wanting*, I have a new appreciation for how desire is created.

Mimetic theory is a lot to unpack. We won't be going into the full details here. But I do want to share a related story that could be helpful.

In 2019, I had the pleasure of finally visiting my personal business mecca; Zingerman's Deli in Ann Arbor, MI.

Longtime readers know I'm a big fan of the business(es) and founder Ari Weinzweig.

Ari was one of the first super successful entrepreneurs I came across who was relentlessly real. You see, a lot of "thought leaders" talk about *past* struggles. But you'll rarely hear them address in real time what they're working on or where their business could do better.

Part of this is the practically-necessary, almost-delusional optimism of any entrepreneur. But nonetheless, it can leave you feeling pretty lonely.

In fact, after my first few years of studying every business book I could get my hands on, I was pretty bummed about how I was doing. Sure, MFF was having pretty unprecedented success in our corner of the industry. Overall, we were doing great work. And we were getting lots of fitness and mainstream media attention.

But I knew I wasn't always delivering as a leader. And I knew our culture had some issues. So instead of basking in the fruits of our labor and reveling in our success, I kept comparing myself to the business books: the stories of businesses with amazing cultures and TED-speaker founders where everyone was happy all the time every second of every day.

And I felt like shit about myself.

So finding Ari's talks on YouTube in 2015 was powerful. Although we wouldn't meet for several more years, he gave me a great gift: he made me feel less alone.

Now flash forward to the time I felt lowest about myself (and MFF).

It was while visiting Zingerman's in 2019.

Huh??

Lemme explain..

I went to take their (excellent!) course on "Training the Trainer." It was great. In fact, we've since hired them to do this training for **the Unicorn Society**.

And visiting the many businesses in the Zingerman's Community of Businesses? Awesome!

I remember sitting in their (so cool!) coffee shop the morning after the seminar. I watched several Zingerman's employees pull up chairs with copies of Ari's books in hand. And I eavesdropped on what appeared to be a semi-informal work session on how Zingerman's could do an even better job of living up to their values.

And for a brief moment, I was so defeated I felt ready to close MFF.

I mean… Zingerman's was like a CITY.

Sure, they'd been at it for 30 years. Admirably, they stressed this in the workshop, as overwhelmed-defeated is probably a semi-common reaction. But still.

What was wrong with me?

Why couldn't I figure out how to make MFF a city?

Why wasn't I a good enough leader to inspire my employees to start their own business underneath the MFF brand?

Why wasn't I good enough to develop my employees so they'd have the chops to succeed with their own businesses?

The obvious answer was, of course, *that I suck*. So perhaps I needed to shut down MFF, move to Ann Arbor, and apply to slice deli meats so I can learn from people who are clearly way smarter than I am?

Sound dramatic?

It felt that way!

I can't say I ever REALLY wanted to shutter MFF. But I really was feeling shitty about myself.

Did I think MFF had more potential? Sure.

Do I *still* think MFF (and BFU and any other business I co-own) has more potential? Sure.

But there is ZERO value in feeling defeated. And it wasn't helpful to compare myself against Zingerman's: a business started more than 20 years before mine, in a completely different industry, in a different part of the country.

Now there IS value in being inspired by what they've created. To look for ideas that spark my passion and get me excited about the future we can create. But that's not how I felt that snowy day in March.

Here's why I'm sharing this with you…

If you're reading this it means two things:

1) You probably own a training gym.

2) You give a shit about having an awesome business.

And that means it's possible that *you too* sometimes compare yourself to other businesses and feel defeated. Maybe you've even done that with MFF.

If so, that's ok. It's ok to feel feelings. It's ok to want more.

AND I'd love to gently nudge you to leverage that energy towards creating the business you want.

Using models for inspiration can serve a place in your development.

But comparison can be the thief of joy.

And you're on your own awesome journey.

And to paraphrase Mikhail Baryshnikov, you'll be best served focusing on *dancing better than yourself.*

Easy Way to Get Reviews

Here's a SUPER easy strategy to implement…

Sometimes members terminate their agreement. And most of the time, they're not runnin' out of the joint cursing you off. (At least I hope.)

The next time you have a member terminating because they're moving or their financial circumstances changed or even because they just want something different…

Ask if they'd be willing to leave you a review.

This may seem like a weird time.

But again, more often than not, they've had a good time training with you. Explain that small businesses live and die by the power of online reviews. Even if your business is no longer a lovematch (for now!), they'll usually be happy to do it as a parting "thank you."

The key here is you want to make this SUPER easy for them.

Be sure to send them a direct link via email and/or text to make it as easy as possible. And consider doing at least one gentle follow-up.

NOTE: This works best when you get a verbal commitment during their exit interview. Otherwise you'll see a meaningfully lower percentage follow through.

NOTE 2: Do an exit interview with terminating members to get feedback, assure them they are still loved, and tell them you hope you'll be seeing them soon. :-)

Time Away From Your Business

Running a training gym is an amazing way to make a living.

You get to do something you love in the service of people you love working alongside people you love.

It doesn't get much better.

However, like anything in life, it's possible to have too much of a good thing.

And we all need some time away. Even if we LOVE what we do. There's simply no way to stay refreshed unless you get time and/or space away from your business.

Beyond physical rest, which is valuable in itself, your brain needs time off so your subconscious can work. This is an important piece of solving big problems and having big ideas.

Here's what this looks like in my life.

At the time of this writing, my first six months of the year have included

- Taking my wife on a babymoon weekend in South Beach
- Spending a long weekend in Marfa, TX looking at modern art and celebrating the birthdays of some dear friends
- Traveling to Atlanta, GA to look into a business opportunity
- Meeting up with friends for a vacation in Morocco
- Following that up with a long weekend in Paris with my wife
- Going back to Miami for a Unicorn Society retreat
- Flying to Chicago so I can spend a full day attending a workshop with Strategic Coach
- Heading to LA for a friend's three-day-long birthday party
- Going back to Chicago for more Strategic Coach
- Flying to Florida for a 4-day entrepreneur retreat
- Heading back to Florida (lots of FL this year) to speak at Perform Better in Orlando

Now this may be more travel than you want. But a few things to consider here:

- If you're someone like me who LOVES travel, there's no words to describe how nourishing this is to my soul.
- You'll notice it's a mix of trips for business and pleasure.
- Some days on the road I unplug from work. Some days I work remotely.
- Much of my best business thinking is done while away from my normal routines. This space is often where I have breakthroughs.
- I know my travel was going to slow down when baby Mark Fisher Fitness arrived. :-)

Now I'm by no means a "passive owner." I'm not taking weeks off at a time, and I usually keep up with emails. And I feel great about this. Because I love my job!

But most training gym owners — even ones who also love their job — don't have this kind of freedom.

So if this stirs a longing in your heart…

Then I want you to have this freedom too.

The way you get there is by developing your skills. Not just as a trainer, but as a business owner who can:

- Reliably grow your business so you have enough revenue that you don't need to do it all alone
- Deliver on your promises with a consistently great experience so your average client sticks around for a while
- Achieve both goals via strong systems and a high-functioning, well-managed team

It's that simple. Not necessarily *easy*. But those are the skills you have to develop to create freedom.

What Should Happen EVERY Session?

We all know that we should have "standard operating procedures" for our training gyms.

But sometimes, this can feel overwhelming. Even the term "standard operating procedure" can sound daunting.

The good news is that if you do this right, it should be simple. After all, we don't want complicated SOP's if no one can remember them. That's not helpful.

Want the *easiest possible way* to start building systems in your training gym?

Start by making sure you have a written set of standards for how you deliver the workout experience.

Make a list of 5-10 things that have to happen in every session for it to be successful.

Some examples include:

- Greet client by name upon entering the training space
- Check in with each client early in the session to see how their body is feeling and help them identify intensity goals for the day
- Use each client's name X times during the session
- Check in halfway through the workout with each client to get feedback from client about how their session is going
- Reference each client's goals at least once during the session while coaching
- Do at least one "name game/icebreaker" during the session
- Give each client a sincere thank you for coming in
- Ask the client when you'll be seeing them next and confirm they have their next session scheduled

The above list may or may not be the correct one for your facility and your culture.

What matters is that there's some manageable sized list of standards. They should be written down, clearly communicated to your coach, and then consistently confirmed to be *actually* happening.

The last point is where this often gets dropped. It's all well and good to have systems, but you have to train your team on the system and keep it top of mind for them.

This means auditing sessions, having your staff audit each other, getting client feedback, or any other number of ways to "inspect what you expect."

Although this example refers to your workout experience, this same gist works for any system in your business. Admittedly, some can get more complicated and may require actual scripts. But the overall idea is the same.

Over time, you'll build up a manual of the SOPs for the various systems in your business. Your team will know what's expected, your clients will get a consistent experience, and all your training gym ownership dreams will come true. :-)

MF's Top Business Books [2022 Updates]

Outside the School of Hard Knocks, synthesizing books is my personal best strategy for upleveling my skills.

I know many of you readers are also... erm... readers.

So it's with great excitement I share the latest update of my list of favorite business books for training gym owners.

This is the third iteration. I hope you'll find some tasty new morsels to add to your list!

Since I will periodically update it, this list is digital.

To check it out, go to businessforunicorns.com/book-stuff

Every Small Business Is Somebody's Dream

Every small business started as somebody's dream.

And many of those dreams were modest. More often than not, the founder just wanted to call her own shots and not have a boss. And the trade-off of increased work hours and extra stress seemed worth it.

But it's not for the faint of heart.

The month-to-month (and year-to-year) income can be erratic in a way that's hard to fathom for someone used to a salary. The small business owner is responsible for drumming up business, hiring and managing other people, and handling an endless parade of surprises. And of course, there are no guarantees. Even a savvy operator is not immune to the slings and arrows of outside circumstances and dumb luck.

But for a lot of people (including yours truly), it's the only way to go.

In the past few decades, the label of "entrepreneur" went from a synonym for "can't get a good job" to carrying a certain amount of sex appeal. Entrepreneurs "disrupt," and "innovate," and take big risks to improve society. And to be fair… there's some truth to this. On balance, entrepreneurs HAVE improved our quality of life with creative products and services.

Now maybe it's because I'm from a lower middle class background in NJ, but I've always stubbornly thought of myself as a "small business owner." I don't bristle if someone refers to me as an entrepreneur. Hell, I use the term because it's one most people use these days. But in my heart of hearts, the label carries a bit of glamor that doesn't ring exactly true for me.

Now, in our own small way, I really do think MFF and BFU are changing the world by changing lives. So it's not that we're without big ambition. But that's the case for most small businesses. You may not read about them in *Fortune*, but these owners work every day to provide amazing service for their clients, create good jobs and a great place to work, and make a good livelihood for their family. And that's why I'm happy to call myself a "proud small business owner."

Challenges aside, the real joy in owning a business has always been the opportunity to positively impact the controllable factors. After all, that's the only part of the game where you have influence. Easier said than done, but no use in stressing about stuff that's out of your hands.

You can't control the cards you were dealt. But you can play the hell out of them to the very best of your ability.

So I guess what I want to say is this:

I appreciate you. And I appreciate *your dream*.

Years, 40 Lessons (Full Text)

Here we are! At the end of the book. You did it!

(Unless you skipped to the end. That's cool too.)

I wanted to share my favorite piece I've written to date. It's a collection of 40 maxims that reflect the most useful frames I have for thinking about business — and for life.

I wrote this piece in January 2020. I'm happy to say, even with allll that's happened since then, it's still an accurate reflection of some of my core guiding principles.

I originally wrote two versions; a short one, and a longer one. However, I think the longer one is infinitely better and richer. As it turns out, almost all maxims suck without context. So that's the one I'm including here.

However, if you prefer the shorter version, you can find it at businessforunicorns.com/book-stuff.

****

As I approached my 40th birthday, I wanted to share some things I've found helpful. In this article, you'll find a hodgepodge of considerations, suggestions, and thinking tools for a better life. After 40 years of thinking, reading, testing, and living, I'm confident the thoughts below will bring you more joy/fulfillment and less suffering/disappointment.

No set of maxims can, or should, shield you completely from adversity; your failures, struggles, and mishaps are what will sharpen the saw of your humanity. But as the saying goes "A smart person learns from their mistakes, a truly wise person learns from the mistakes of others."

Some of these thoughts represent a radical departure from what I would have said on the eve of my 30th birthday. I suspect after ten more years of life these will further evolve, as they should. But for now, consider these musings some of my "Notes From The Road So Far."

New DECADE... let's GO!!!!

****

1) No maxims are 100% correct in all contexts.

For any maxim/principle, including all the ones listed here, one can always find contexts where it would be incorrect.

Virtually all maxims have an implicit qualification: "But of course, there are obvious exceptions." Or as the statisticians say, "All models are wrong, some are useful." Many people discount the maxim because they can think of an exception. This is silly, because you can find an exception to all maxims.

It's useful to observe where/when the maxim/principle doesn't apply. But it's probably more useful to identify the circumstances under which would be correct.

RELATED: For an "all-purpose" maxim to be helpful, it should be correct 90-99% of the time. Otherwise it's not a very good maxim. UNLESS you add a qualifier to stipulate the context in which it's correct.

Social media is full of aspiring thought leaders making pronouncements without context that are correct 40-60% of the time. I never know if the individual is constrained by their attempt at brevity, or genuinely sees the situation in black or white. In these situations, I give people the benefit of the doubt.

2) When there's something you want that you don't have or can't get, there's something you don't know.

Sometimes what you don't know is *how* to apply knowledge. And sometimes there's a mindset problem. But ultimately, if you're not getting the results you want, you're missing part of the puzzle.

If you're not happy with an area of your life, invest time, energy, and money in studying that area.

This goes for pretty much anything. Relationships, money, fitness, marketing, management, happiness… if you're not happy with your results, there are already solutions out there and people who are masters of those domains. It's unwise to bang your head against the wall trying to figure it all out on your own. It's also unwise to bury your head in the sand, though this can be a common response when we're struggling so much with a given topic that it's painful.

Buy some books, find out who the experts are, look into conferences and coaches, do some Googling, search on YouTube, etc. etc. etc.

3) If you want to be successful in life and business, you've got to get the incentives right.

This goes for you personally, for your team, for your clients/ customers, and for your society.

And that's *damn hard*, because whenever you incentivize a given outcome, you're also creating second and third order consequences. For instance, in a famous example from colonial India, Delhi had a cobra problem. The British governor decided to pay people for turning in cobra heads to help reduce the cobra count. And... people started *actively breeding cobras* to have more to turn in and collect the reward. Womp womp.

Furthermore, in many situations, adding incentives can backfire by reducing motivation. Check out Daniel Pink's *Drive*.

However, if you have NO incentives, you don't have any influence on behaviors. No one has "skin in the game" and you're not leveraging the power of enlightened self-interest.

Think a few steps ahead, then do your best. It's usually not possible to create a perfect system, but you can still create one that's "good enough."

4a) "The most important ability is dependability." - Zig Ziglar

People who always follow through on what they say they're going to do are very rare. And what is rare is valuable.

There are many reasons for this. But in my experience, most people just don't have a reliable system for keeping track of the things they say they're going to do. And if you have any complexity in your life, your memory won't cut it unless you write it down somewhere AND have a system to process your tasks.

Few things lay a better foundation for personal and professional success than being dependable. When you become known as the person who everyone can always count on, you become infinitely more valuable. You don't have to spend time healing damaged trust after broken promises. And you don't have to be closely "managed," so it takes less bandwidth and energy to work with you because you keep yourself accountable.

Being dependable doesn't require any special talent. But it does require caring enough to develop some system for organizing your commitments and deadlines. Admittedly, not everyone naturally takes to this sort of organization. But the payoff is HUGE: better relationships, more professional opportunities, more trust, more responsibility, more freedom, and more income.

4b) "Self esteem is your reputation with yourself." - Naval Ravikant

Like all maxims, this is mostly correct, "but of course there are obvious exceptions." Yes, sometimes low self-esteem is a result of trauma, socialization, or something that requires the support of a clinician like a therapist. Sometimes there's even something going on physiologically that may benefit from medication.

But on balance, for most people, your self-esteem is a reflection of your reputation with yourself. Can you rely on *yourself* to do what you commit to do? Do you keep your commitments with *yourself*? Even the little ones, like getting up without repeatedly hitting the alarm? Do you have a track record of good faith effort and genuinely doing your very best most days?

If not, it's a good place to start if you'd like to improve your self-esteem. To be successful, you'll have to become proficient at "playing games you can win" and being realistic about your commitments to yourself. You'll also need a heaping dose of self-compassion with your inevitable breaches.

But if you go to bed most nights knowing you really did your best that day, your probability of being satisfied with yourself will be much, much higher.

5) Don't care too much about what other people think. But it's ok and ideal to care some.

And you should weigh how much you care based on how certain you are that their opinion is credible in that domain.

"Fuck the haters" is a silly philosophy. Sometimes haters make accurate (if painful) observations.

However, it is also silly to give your power away willy nilly. Because you'll never please everyone. And if you have any level of success, you WILL have rocks thrown at you.

A related thought:

6) Feedback is just data.

When you receive feedback, it's your job to look it over and decide if it's true or not. Carefully considering the merit of feedback is superior to automatically dismissing it because of poor delivery OR you dislike the messenger OR because it makes you upset OR etc. etc. etc.

However, carefully considering the merit of feedback is ALSO superior to taking all feedback to heart, being reactive, solving problems you don't have, giving away your personal power, etc. etc. etc.

Most feedback is bad. First of all, most people deliver it poorly. Second of all, many people aren't clear thinkers and can't see outside their own desires and interests. Third of all, their feedback is always based on a very limited bit of information about your behaviors. They have no real knowledge of your intentions, behaviors they didn't see, etc.

However, it's still a gift to add someone else's perspective to your own. Even if you ultimately disagree, you have more insight to how you, or your business, is being perceived. And that's a valuable data point.

On average, I estimate about 70% of the feedback I get about Mark Fisher Fitness or Business for Unicorns is not actionable or incorrect. But think about it logically. Even with a 30% batting average, that's still LOTS of helpful ideas. Also worth noting: leaving aside internet trolls, when a client or customer takes the time to share their feedback with you, it means they're invested in your success. And that is awesome! You are lucky! They are cool! It may not always *feel* like it, but see Maxim 31.

It's also important to understand how sensitive you are to feedback. If feedback is scary and feels like a punch in the throat, you likely need to underweight it. Take time before you take action or you may needlessly overreact and solve problems that don't really exist. On the other hand, if you don't understand why everyone's so tightly wound all the time and you only have a passing curiosity in what others think/feel, you may be an UNDER responder. This too could lead to subpar decision making.

When you begin to get truly curious to understand feedback about you and/or your business, you're on the way to expedited growth/learning.

Read *Thanks for the Feedback* by Douglas Stone and Sheila Heen and *Persuadable: How Great Leaders Change Their Minds to Change the World* by Al Pittampalli.

7) It's particularly helpful to be able to learn from people that are not your cup of tea.

People you don't like and/or who dislike you are uniquely well positioned to help you discover things that aren't obvious to you. It's BECAUSE they're unlike you that they hold so much value for you.

You may still disagree. But if you can resist the impulse to discount/dismiss, you have an opportunity to learn things you won't discover when studying those with similar values, personal style, philosophies, etc. See Maxim 30.

However:

8) Be wary of cynics.

Sometimes you can get helpful feedback from cynics. But people that fundamentally distrust the sincerity and integrity of most/all humans have a warped frame. Keep this in mind.

They (usually) mean well. But in their attempts to protect themselves and/or make sense of being let down, their worldview is as skewed, unhelpful, and potentially dangerous as naive Pollyannas.

Consider their perspective and look for helpful takeaways. But remember their frame generally prevents them from thinking critically and seeing clearly.

9) Pretty much everybody could benefit from therapy of some kind.

Unless you made it out of your childhood and adolescence without any wounds.

Now not everyone *needs* therapy. But pretty much everyone would benefit. This is analogous to *physical* therapy. Not everyone necessarily needs one, but a good physical therapist can do things that a fitness trainer can't. Skilled therapists have helpful tools; though admittedly, personal fit to both therapist AND modality of course play a role.

You'll just suffer less. And that's not purely a selfish consideration. When you suffer less, you'll be a better version of you for the people you love and the world at large.

Also worth considering:

10) Work on yourself some. But not too much.

This one is tricky, as each individual will have to decide what's "too little" or "too much."

As a rule of thumb, people that love love LOVE self-work/personal development/retreats/elaborate journaling prompts, etc. *may* be at risk of doing too much. People that find all that stuff to be mostly bullshit are at risk of doing too little.

It's fair to say if you're not spending any time on yourself via coaching, therapy, personal development, etc., you're likely not growing as a human. A commitment to growth is a non-negotiable trait for me in potential friends, business partners, and team members. Complacency breeds bored and boring)humans. (CONGRATS… you're reading this, there's a 99% probability you pass this bar!)

Conversely, and less discussed, it's possible to do *too much* work on yourself.

It's possible for self-work to take up a disproportionate amount of resources past the point of diminishing returns. This can displace/ impede action-taking.

There's no algorithm for this, really, but a good proxy is the amount of time spent "sharpening your saw" measured against the amount of time "using your saw." Working on yourself is valuable, but at some point you have to engage in the world, with other people, and with society. I don't know the exact ratio, and as usual, context always matters. But there IS a tipping point.

For many people, self work can become a great justification for avoiding *doing the damn thing* and putting themselves out there/ shipping their work. Furthermore, many modalities of self-work require breaking yourself down, asking yourself hard questions, and focusing on/looking for the areas that are not working well. This is very useful in the right dose. But if you do LOTS and LOTS and LOTS of this, you may become neurotic, self-doubting, and incapable of taking action in a quixotic quest to become "ready."

11) "Your weaknesses are your strengths taken to their extremes." - Ari Weinzweig

This little nugget is from one of my heroes, Ari Weinzweig of Zingerman's Deli in Ann Arbor, MI.

This is an important consideration. Particularly because by definition, if you're capable of creating extreme results, you likely have some extreme tendencies. Be mindful of how far you're pushing your strengths. They can come out the back door and bite you in the ass.

12) To be fulfilled, focus on two things: being a Student and being a Servant.

When uncertain what to do with your morning/day/life, learning things and/or serving people will be a satisfying choice.

I aspire to be a Student every day. By nature, I'm intrinsically curious as hell. I love to learn. But I also know being a Student is necessary for me to be a *good* Servant. I aspire to be a Student of 1) the World and 2) Myself. I need to know and understand both. I'll never have perfect knowledge, but the more useful knowledge, skills, and wisdom I develop, the more effective I can be as a Servant.

Conversely, I can't be a truly great Student unless I'm an aspiring Servant. If I'm learning in a vacuum and never synthesizing/sharing/utilizing, I'm not actually completing the final step of learning.

If I'm awake, I think it's fun to be learning things and serving people.

BONUS: The best and most foundational form of Service is unconditional positive regard: acceptance, compassion, and sincere love. Hard to do, but a worthwhile goal.

A related and paradoxical thought:

13) It's a trap to define your self-worth purely in terms of what you can do for other people.

DOING is important to a good life. As Earl Nightingale said, "Happiness is the progressive realization of a worthy goal or idea."

And while that's true, this has to be balanced against the value of simply BEING. This isn't to say one should resist the human urge for growth, progress, self-actualization, achievement, etc. It IS to say that one should also spend some dedicated time doing nothing, being bored, wandering, schedule-less, at Burning Man, etc.

This past year I took more time to simply "be" than any other year of my adult life. Since I can, at times, wrap my feelings of self-worth up in my value to others, this was occasionally challenging. It's honorable to want to contribute to a better world. But high-achieving strivers also benefit from taking time to be still.

Yes, this will refresh your brain. You'll come back with more creativity and energy and laterally-attained ideas.

But spending time simply BEING isn't just a *means* to more effective DOING.

It's an end unto itself.

BONUS: This is part of the value of a meditation practice. It's a consistent and daily commitment to spending part of my day just BEING.

14) Happiness is best created by (spending time, energy, and money on) experiences and relationships, not things.

The human brain is wired to want "stuff." Our society and its sophisticated marketing machinery expertly fans these flames.

BUT research (and common sense) has shown very conclusively that happiness doesn't come from acquiring stuff. It comes from experiences and meaningful relationships. So if choosing between buying an expensive designer luxury thingamaroo or going on a weekend vacation with a partner or dear friend, it's usually best to choose the latter.

15) A disciplined gratitude practice is the most reliable intervention to improve your mental well-being.

Scientists currently believe up to 50% of one's happiness is determined by a genetic set-point.

And while happiness is not necessarily the mark of a life well-lived, people with good attitudes tend to be more effective. However our brains tend to focus on what's going wrong and ruminate, often on negative things that are out of our power to control.

Creating some daily habits around appreciating the things that ARE going well in your life is a powerful way to slowly rewire your brain. You'll still see negative things. That's not only ok, it's desirable; this can help spur action and identify opportunities for improvement.

If you tend to overweight the negative and rarely appreciate what's going well, take some time each day to identify what you're grateful for.

BONUS: When you feel gratitude towards a *person*, let them know. And tell them why. Perhaps in a handwritten card.

"Feeling gratitude for someone and not expressing it is like wrapping a present but never giving it." - Andrew Horn, founder of Tribute.

PS Tribute is a very cool company that makes it super easy to make video montages of appreciation to celebrate humans you love. Check out tribute.co.

16) If you're not sure what you want in a situation, ask yourself what you DON'T want. That will probably be more obvious. Then explore the *opposite* of what you DON'T want.

"Invert, always invert." - Carl Jacobi

This is one of my favorite thinking tools, commonly called "inversion." Many people do this intuitively BUT ineffectively. Since it's so easy to articulate and focus on what you DON'T want, that's as far as many people get. They spend their time and energy thinking about, discussing, and 85% focusing on what they DON'T want. The key is to use this knowledge to focus on what you DO want.

Feeling stuck? Ask yourself the magic question:

"How would you like this to be different?"

BONUS STRATEGY: If you're not sure how to get what you want, identify the OPPOSITE of what you want. Then identify how you'd need to behave to create the OPPOSITE of what you want. Then identify the opposite of *those* behaviors.

Example: If you're not sure how to have a great marriage, consider how you'd need to behave to have a horrible marriage. What are the OPPOSITE of the behaviors that would create a horrible marriage? It's likely some of them would be helpful in creating a great marriage.

While he didn't invent inversion, I attribute my purposeful application of this tool to Charlie Munger. He's one of my heroes.

17) To increase your probability of achieving a goal, first decide on exactly what you want. Then track stuff.

You'll be best off tracking both inputs (behaviors, processes) and outputs (outcomes, results), though sometimes focusing on behaviors alone is sufficient.

For example, if you want your business to make a certain amount of money, it's a good idea to create a specific number goal with a target date. Then track the weekly, daily, or monthly activities that will contribute to that goal AND track the results along the way so you know if you need to change course.

Sometimes people say weird stuff like "goal setting doesn't work, focus on systems." That's a weird thing to say. A good goal setting system 1) should include systems for getting your goal and 2) should be realistic about the goal evolving over time. They're not mutually exclusive.

That said, depending on the goal, sometimes you *are* best focusing purely on behaviors. This is usually the intention behind statements like "goal setting doesn't work." For instance, when it comes to my health and fitness, I'm not particularly focused on my weight or body fat percentage or any particular performance goals. While I'm not without vanity, I mostly care about brain function, happiness, and longevity. And my long term health is the ultimate delayed feedback loop; it doesn't have clear daily outcomes for me to track, at least not at this age. So for my health and fitness goals, I simply focus on "core self-care" behaviors.

There are fancy apps for this, but I personally use a Google Sheet with conditional formatting. I keep it open on my "home" set of browser tabs, along with my email inboxes and calendar. Then I update it throughout the day. The cell turns green if I hit it, and red if I don't. This provides a dopamine hit of satisfaction for completing my habit. This in turn creates a positive reinforcement feedback loop for activities that aren't intrinsically satisfying.

Since adopting this in Oct. 2018, it's been remarkable how easy it is to finally adopt habits. Whether it's cutting back on drinking, flossing daily, meditating, or warming up before lifting, it seems all I need to do is log it and... BAM! I suddenly find myself doing it far more regularly.

Shoot me an email at mark@businessforunicorns.com if you want me to share a screenshot with you.

NOTE: Clarity on your goals does not guarantee you will achieve them.

However, NOT having any clear goals makes it very unlikely that you'll *accidentally* stumble into the life of your dreams.

And now... a counter thought.

18) What gets measured gets managed. But you can't always measure what matters.

Many important things in life are not easily quantifiable. That doesn't mean they don't matter. Sometimes/often they matter more.

Be mindful of "The Tyranny of the Quantifiable": the sneaky impulse of your brain to accidentally prioritize goals that can be quantified over things that are *actually* more impactful for a good life. The classic example here is chasing money over satisfying relationships.

In some contexts, using subjective ratings can be a helpful workaround (e.g. organizational morale surveys, ranking your satisfaction in your marriage, etc. etc. etc.). The Net Promoter Score is a good numerical number to track for customer satisfaction.

For more customer service stuff, check out our online learning platform, Unicorn University, where you will find courses like ***Clients for Life.*** More information at businessforunicorns.com/book-stuff.

19) The best time management skill is the ability to do one thing at a time without letting yourself get distracted.

It's relatively easy to set up a work session to avoid *external* distractions. You can take push notifications off your phone, put it on "do not disturb," tell your colleagues not to interrupt you during certain periods of focused work, close your door, etc.

The bigger issue for most of us is *internal* distractions; we've been trained by our phones to get "itchy" when we're working on something for more than a few minutes. Many of us will feel a pull to check our email, or check social media, or pretty much do ANYTHING that will take us away from the work at hand. This isn't a recipe for doing focused high quality work.

Consider using the "Pomodoro Technique" and set an alarm for 25 minutes of uninterrupted focus followed by a five minute break. These short, intentional sprints can help override your "itches" because you know you have a break coming. Additionally, giving your brain a break every 25 minutes is a good best practice to maximize your creativity/productivity over the course of a day. I also suspect this practice can help train your brain to remain on task for more than a few minutes at time.

Related Thought: Personal tech is ubiquitous; this is great AND horrible.* Although we've gained some convenience, many of us now let our work life bleed into our recreational activities or our time with loved ones. Instead of relaxing and being present, we've trained our brains to constantly look for diversions. Consider taking a weekly 24 hour break from digital diversions.

If you want more stuff like this, check out our online learning platform, Unicorn University, where you will find our time management course ***Time Ninja,*** and other courses like it. More information at businessforunicorns.com/book-stuff.

*Another way tech is horrible: we're trading away privacy for convenience. This will be one of the biggest issues of the next decade as we slowly start to understand the ramifications.

20) Good time management is about weaponizing smart laziness.

I'm better at time management than most people because I'm very, very lazy. This often strikes people as false modesty. A lot of people think I'm a hard worker and highly productive. And I am. But being a hard worker/highly productive and being lazy are NOT mutually exclusive. In fact the latter is the key to the former.

I basically don't want to do anything unless 1) it's really moving me towards my goals (as a Student and Servant) and 2) I *truly* have to be the one to personally do it.

Most people spend too much time on shit that doesn't matter. And they're too reluctant/slow/unskilled at delegating and getting things off their plate.

Even if it only takes me 60 seconds to do, I'll happily spend 30 seconds to write an email to delegate the task.

Seconds make minutes make hours make days.

And the days may be long, but the years are short.

And now, an inversion:

21) Few things will impede a successful life more than a tireless commitment to becoming world class at *shit that doesn't actually matter.*

It's helpful to be able to put your head down and get to work. But you will get nowhere fast unless you learn how to prioritize based on your long term goals and your personal values.

The essence of effective strategy is identifying what you're NOT going to do. Minimize tasks and projects that don't have massive impact and move you towards the life you want.

You will never get it all done. Particularly in today's day and age. Eliminate the non-essential.

"Less but better." - Dieter Rams

22) Conventional intelligence is just table stakes. Unless combined with the ability to consistently produce work AND emotional intelligence, it will not lead to success.

The world is filled with hyper-intelligent people who are professionally and personally unsuccessful. There are two main reasons for this.

First, success is not just about how you THINK or your IDEAS, it's about what you DO. Surely the latter benefits from clear thinking; to the extent that it helps you make good choices, more intellectual firepower is better than less. *But you still have to do stuff to get results*. And many productive people of average intelligence with "just ok" ideas outperform geniuses that spend their time lost in thought.

Second, if you have lots of brainpower but minimal emotional intelligence, you're generally going to have big problems. In some cases, you can mitigate this by working with someone who can leverage your brains while protecting the world from you. And to be fair, if you do execute well, you can absolutely still have some professional success. But not only will this deficit set limits on your professional success, you will pay a real price in your personal life.

Brains alone are not enough. Commit to actually getting things done AND to life long learning about interpersonal skills.

If you need help with the latter, you can improve if you work on it. We offer coaching on emotional intelligence.

23) Training, delegating, and managing other people are non-negotiable skills if you want to maximize your output and impact on the world.

Otherwise your output and impact will always be limited by your personal time, energy, and skill capacity.

Consider taking a "Training the Trainer" course. Learn how to effectively teach your team how to execute the systems that create your desired outcomes. Commit to become a world class delegator. Study the art of management/leadership.

BONUS: Studying practical psychology is a good foundation for this work.If you don't understand how people are wired, what they value, what motivates them, etc., you won't build the positive relationships necessary for success.

If you'd like to learn more about these skills, check out our online learning platform, Unicorn University, where you will find our course on leadership and building a team, ***The Care and Feeding of Superheroes*** and others like it. More information on businessforunicorns.com/book-stuff.

I know some very successful people who have a lot of stress/

suffering in their life because of constant turmoil in their professional relationships.

A similar but related idea: Become a lifelong learner about technical automation. More and more things will be automated every single year. But until the robots *really* take over, mastering the art of training, delegating, and managing other people will always be a foundational skill for those who want to make a big impact.

24) "Never attribute to malice what can adequately be explained by stupidity or incompetence." - Hanlon's Razor

Since your brain is wired to create patterns AND be wary of cheats, most humans are on the lookout for villainy. But we tend to assign poor motives and unchanging character flaws when usually the person just doesn't know what the fuck they're doing and/or is being lazy or thoughtless. This results in unnecessary suffering: for *you*.

And if you happen to be a manager of the individual in question, it's a great way to poison the relationship. It will ensure that the accountability conversation leaves them accurately feeling judged and misunderstood. Another common and painful truth: in many situations, the reason they failed was inadequate training/ coaching on your part.

A related customer service mantra: "Better naïveté than paranoia."

Everyone's doing the best they can from where they are. Even though that may objectively be shitty.

Everyone's fighting a battle. Be kind.

25) You can be a great human without being a great leader. But you can't be a great leader without being a great human.

Being a wonderful human being with great interpersonal skills and a keen eye for detail doesn't necessarily mean you're going to be a successful leader. There are other skills that have to be stacked.

But if you master the skills of leadership without having done the requisite work on yourself as a person, you'll always have a ceiling. Based on the organization, this may or may not impact your short term financial results. Admittedly, in many perverse scenarios, being a good human can sometimes prevent the best possible short term financial results.

But if the goal is the best possible *long term* financial results AND a culture where people are growing and feel valued and cared for… the mechanics of leadership alone aren't going to cut it.

You have to be the kind of person that other high quality humans are willing to follow.

26) There is no such thing as a universally effective leader in all situations. And certainly not for all people.

Leadership is VERY contextual. Different situations, organizations, and goals all require different approaches. The best leaders know how to be flexible and adapt their style to the situation at hand. But since leaders are only human, they will naturally have modes of operation that are more comfortable and intuitive.

This is why a leader can thrive in one business and be a bust in another. It's also why the person who starts an organization isn't always the one who can lead it through various stages of growth.

27a) Learn how to write (sufficiently) well.

I don't see a world in which the need for adequate writing goes away. Yes, more and more communication will happen via video. But writing has benefits that video does not, and it will remain more practical for many kinds of communication.

You can get better at this. Read books like *Bird by Bird: Some Instructions on Writing and Life* by Anne Lamott, *The Elements of F*cking Style: A Helpful Parody* by Chris Baker, etc. Take a class or a course on it.

You don't even need to be great. At a certain point, for most life skills, there's diminishing returns after a certain level of competence. I'm an adequate writer at best. But I AM able to communicate quickly, concisely, warmly, and clearly. And without exaggeration, this "just good enough" skill is the parent of much of my professional success.

BONUS #1: Learn how to communicate via emails in particular. For the foreseeable future, they will be an important part of professional communication. Learn to organize your thoughts clearly and with good formatting to clients, co-workers, partners, etc.

BONUS #2: Learn how to type quickly. If you can't type *at least* 60 words per minute, upgrade this skill. If you spend any time typing, and you almost certainly do if you're reading this, this is a *small hinge* that will open a *huge door*.

27b) Learn how to speak sufficiently well.

While writing matters in many contexts, at the risk of stating the stupidly obvious, much important communication will happen via conversation. Sales pitches, "sales" pitches writing up a team member, having a difficult conversation with a loved one, giving a speech to a group of people, articulating your love for someone you adore… these are important skills.

This is why everyone benefits from studying public speaking. Whether you actually speak in front of groups of people or not, it's a highly transferable skill.

Unlike writing, this is one of my marquee skills. I have chosen to combine my natural talent, interest, and years of experience as a professional actor with disciplined ongoing study and effort towards incremental improvement. This may or may not make sense for you. But it will behoove you to become *at least* adequate.

I also recommend signing up for Toastmasters.

28) We are ALL in sales. We are all "Agents of Influence."

Many people find the very word "sales" to be repugnant. Same with "marketing."

And this makes sense. But what we all despise is low-integrity, high-pressure sales that don't actually have more than a passing interest in what you actually need or want. Unfortunately, since most of us have experienced this in our lives, the word is scorched earth.

But effectively supporting people in taking action doesn't require being shady. In fact, doing it well necessitates genuine care and concern. It's appropriate to acknowledge there are other incentives at play, and any salesperson is incentivized financially and/or professionally to convince people to pay for a given service.

But at the end of the day, every human has desires that require "selling" other people on a shared vision and parting with resources: time, money, and energy. You may be "selling" your child on finishing their homework. Or "selling" your mom on recycling. Or "selling" your boss on giving you a bigger raise.

The keys to doing it with integrity and doing it well:

1. Genuinely caring about the individual you're influencing.
2. Sincerely believing your proposed plan of action is actually in their long term best interest.
3. A deep respect for their autonomy in making their own decisions.

29) Intellectual humility – coupled with the right dose of introspection – is the foundation to continued personal and professional growth.

The moment you have it all figured out is usually the death of further growth. Or at the least, it's a moment of "pride before the fall."

To be clear, it is possible to be *overly* introspective. Too much time spent questioning yourself can lead to subpar action-taking, which is always where real learning happens. But one probably can't be too humble, provided you're continually taking action on what seems to be true, while leaving the door open to having your beliefs challenged.

"The first principle is you must not fool yourself – and you are the easiest person to fool." - Richard Feynman

30) "Seek first to understand." Particularly when mad, hurt, confused, offended, etc.

This is perhaps the most powerful of all of Stephen Covey's *7 Habits of Highly Effective People.*

A curious, open mind is always a good look. It's particularly valuable when emotions are involved. While emotions are important, they have a way of clouding your understanding. When you are upset with someone else, or perhaps more importantly, when they are upset with *you*, sincerely seek to understand where they're coming from. It will benefit both you personally and the relationship.

31) Emotions are vital, helpful, and often slightly flawed tools for understanding our preferences and driving decision making.

We don't want to deny or ignore our emotions. And we should be realistic that total conscious control isn't possible, or frankly, desirable. But we also don't want to assume our emotions always lead to good decisions without at least some oversight.

There's a reasonable debate over how much control people actually have over their emotions. It's pretty clear we have at least *some* influence over how we feel about things; on the other hand, it's also clear no one has complete self-mastery of their emotional responses. Emotions function largely unconsciously. Most humans can relate to feeling something we knew wasn't logical, and yet couldn't shake the physical sensation. It can sometimes seem like there are two of us in our brains.

Social psychologist Jonathan Haidt discusses this conflict in his excellent book *The Happiness Hypothesis*. Haidt refers to these two different "selves" as the Rider (our thinking, logic brain) and the Elephant (our powerful, emotional brain).

While emotions sometimes get a bad rap, we quite literally can't make decisions without them. Like many things in life, we just want to find a sweet spot. We don't want wild swings of emotion that result in impulsive behavior that moves us away from what we actually want most. Conversely, we don't want desperate repression in a doomed attempt to be creatures of pure logic with no knowledge of or language for our emotional life.

What we want is a richly explored inner life that never makes emotions "wrong"; we fully accept, observe, and *feel our feelings*. We tune into the physical sensations they bring. We get curious about what our emotions are telling us. We find productive ways to process our feelings, often in conversation with supportive people and/or through physical exertion. But we also know our emotional responses are sometimes a well-intentioned but outdated defense mechanism. Or a completely reasonable response to an honest misunderstanding or miscommunication. And we know that in the very least, when we find ourselves overcome with emotion, it's usually not when we're doing our very best thinking.

Your heart matters AND your brain matters. As is often the case, *we want both*.

32) An addiction to being "right" often prevents people from getting *what they really want*.

This one is HYOOOGE.

Every time you feel your ego flare up during a disagreement, you're slipping into an unhelpful place; it's a warning sign you're about to start arguing why you're "right" and trying to "win." You'll stop seeking to understand. You'll be unwilling to genuinely consider if you're wrong. An opportunity to learn will be lost. And more than likely the quality of the relationship is going to take a hit.

When you find yourself in conflict with someone else, which is normal and often valuable, always zoom out and make sure you're clear on what you actually want most.

33) Be cautious when you have strong opinions about topics you don't actually know much about.

Questions are great. Theories are great. But strong and forcefully held opinions – with no knowledge base or track record of results in a given domain – are the source of much human suffering.

Sure, many fields benefit from the perspective of an outsider. It's entirely possible you are able to intuit something because you don't know "the rules." But this can usually be offered with questions and theories. It doesn't require the near certainty of forcefully held opinions.

This is all the trickier for smart and articulate people who've had success of some kind. When people look to you as a "thought leader" and your brain works very fast, you're at risk of overstepping. When you're asked a question about something you don't actually know much about, you might immediately formulate a credible sounding answer and start spewing bullshit without even realizing it.

There are huge swaths of the human experience that are not being commented on in these maxims. Some just didn't make the cut. But most are topics I'm frankly not qualified to comment on.

34) Healthy conflict is the secret sauce to leveraging the power of groups. If you do this right, two plus two will equal *five*.

Without conflict, there's no growth. In any community/organization, the quality of thinking improves by marrying different perspectives and ironing out the conflict.

At some point, a leader has to make a subjective call about where to steer the ship, even if consensus hasn't been reached. But to make the best decision *requires* vetting conflicting viewpoints.

"When two people in business always agree, one is unnecessary."

35) The Law of Attraction may or may not actually be true.

Regardless, it's a good way to approach your life and work.

It's entirely possible the Law of Attraction is just a trick of the mind that makes you *feel* like you're drawing people and circumstances to you that are aligned with what you think and feel. But it sure *feels* like I'm creating my own reality most days.

Are there actually esoteric metaphysical currents of energy stirring the cosmic soup in the direction of your thoughts/feelings? No idea. But it's logically a useful strategy to focus on what you DO want. To greet your day like a happy warrior, confidently and boldly moving in the direction of your dreams.

To be clear… "When you pray, move your feet." I'm not saying you should buy something you can't afford and then *manifest* the money. I AM saying a commitment to the tenets of the Law of Attraction – factually true or not – will lead to better outcomes. You'll likely do better work, you'll be more creative/flexible, you'll have more fun, people will like being around you more, etc. etc.

"You become what you think about most of the time" may sound woowoo, but I think it's logical.

36) Authenticity is poorly understood, and possibly overrated.

This one is potentially provocative, so allow me to unpack…

What we DON'T want is to be fake, forced, disingenuous, conniving, etc. But is the opposite of these traits "authenticity?"

It depends on how you define it. While "being true to yourself" is a generally decent principle, what if your "authentic self" just doesn't feel like paying taxes? Or what if you "authentically" want to eat ice cream every night?

Let's say you choose to write me unsolicited feedback about this book. Logically, I know your intentions are good. But I don't know you. Furthermore, your reasoning has obvious and objective flaws. So my first impulse to unsolicited feedback is to dislike you for overstepping AND respond with a curt, dismissive comment pointing out your flaws in reasoning. Am I "out of my integrity" if I don't honor my inner spirit's intuition? Which is to judge you as a nitpicker who didn't read the 1st maxim? Is it ok if I beat you over the head with my copy of *Daring Greatly* while reciting the Roosevelt quote about the man in the arena?

The challenge with "authenticity" is that humans are complicated. We have many layers and many sides. Furthermore, while we have genetic wiring and natural inclinations, we — the many versions of us — are also a product of our own self-creation. And sometimes what *feels* like your intuition is just your fear and desire for self-preservation dressed up in a tuxedo.

Again, this isn't an argument for being fake, forced, disingenuous, conniving, etc. It's simply acknowledging that "authenticity" is a nebulous concept since it implies there's a *true you*. In fact... you "contain multitudes." And you're forever in the process of (re)creating yourself.

CONCESSION: Advice to "be authentic" is well-intentioned and can be helpful in some situations ("But of course there are obvious exceptions"). Particularly when it refers to exploring what you *really* want, what you *really* feel, what you *really* think, etc.

37) We are ALL practical moral philosophers.

Admittedly, some of us spend more time thinking about our impact on the world than others. Not everyone spends their free time creating thought experiments to consider how best to balance equality and liberty. Frankly, many people don't seem to give a shit about this kind of stuff at all.

But by being a human and having any opinion whatsoever on – or taking part in – a business, a community, marriages, family, politics, social justice, the government, the law, power dynamics, etc.... you DO have ethical intuitions.

Now some people have more or less explicit interest in moral philosophy and the study of ethics. Some people have beliefs that have been deeply examined and are endlessly evolving. Others haven't thought much more deeply beyond what they were taught by their families and high schools.

But if we're a part of any of the above systems, as we all are, we're making choices every single day. So although it may seem strange, we are all practitioners of moral philosophy.

And that's why I think it's good to spend at least some time thinking about it.

38) Choosing the right people to build a life with will do much to mitigate suboptimal decision making and bad luck.

Conversely, you can do almost everything "correct" to create the life you want, and yet have your happiness totally thwarted by poor choices of spouse, business partner(s), teammates, etc.

This is as obvious as it is vitally important.

39) Health really is the first wealth.

At the end of the day, health is the foundation of *everything*. But one of the biggest challenges with health and longevity is the feedback loop is massively delayed. You can "get away" with neglecting your health and fitness… for a while. Sometimes for years. And genetics are certainly a part of the equation, to good and ill effect.

But you will spend time, energy, and money on your health and fitness at some point in your life. The more time you're willing to spend on proactive measures, the higher probability you'll experience long term robust health and fitness.

BONUS: There is LOTS of debate about the best way to pursue fitness. As most readers will know, my other business, Mark Fisher Fitness, is devoted entirely to helping people find the path that works for them. But at the risk of being totally reductionistic, some non-controversial guidelines:

- Eat a reasonable amount of mostly non-processed, perishable single-ingredient foods that you actually like. Emphasize plants.

- Get in some kind of physical activity that you actually like at least several times a week, ideally every day.

- Take sleep hygiene seriously. Strive for 7-8 hours a night.

- Cultivate self care rituals that nourish you: walks in nature, meditation, prayer, reading, etc.

- Find work you genuinely enjoy/love. If that's not possible, at least find work you don't hate.

- Spend time every with people you love and who love you back.

Final thought: remember you are *robust*. During a season of career focus (or young children!), you may not nail all of the above. Do your best. Accept it won't be perfect.

But also be honest about the difference between a temporary disruption and an indefinite lifestyle that needs an intervention.

40) Memento Mori.

Remember you will die.

This is one of my superpowers. Like some of you reading this, I had a brush with death in my teenage years that forever changed me, mostly for the good. But I admit it *does* get in my way at times if I'm not being careful (see 11).

In fact, one of the most meaningful experiences of my year was a health scare. Everything turned out ok, but I was completely and totally rocked (see 39). I'm grateful for the experience, as it forced me to address the dark side of this superpower. It was also the impetus to finally start therapy (see 9). But on balance, I believe a healthy awareness of mortality has always been my secret sauce. It powers my bias for action and the joyful urgency with which I approach my work AND my fun. More days than not, I *bound* out of bed in the morning. And this is because I don't take my life for granted.

From one of my favorite websites/blogs:

"The goal of personal growth should be deathbed clarity while your life is still happening so you can actually do something about it." - WaitButWhy.com

Thank You

Thanks again for coming on this journey and reading my reflections about life and running a successful training gym.

Remember, you can download more resources at businessforunicorns.com/book-stuff.

And if you like my musings, here are three other (free) resources to get more MF and Business for Unicorns magic…

MarkFisherYouTube.com - This is my YouTube channel. It's my very favorite thing I get to do. If you like reading my words, you may like hearing me say words while watching my face move (*a lot*). You will learn stuff and hopefully get some LOLs.

GymOwnerReportCard.com - Do you ever feel a bit overwhelmed about *all* the things you need to do in order to run your training gym? That makes sense! This is a really cool tool that will help you identify how you're doing in each of the core functions of running your training gym.

BusinessForUnicorns.com/Podcast - This is our podcast. You'll get to hear myself, Michael Keeler, Pete Dupuis, Ben Pickard, and a whole array of fitness business smartypants peeps. Subscribe to us on your preferred podcast app and we shall beam fitness knowledge directly into your earholes.

Also, you can follow me on **@markfisherhumanbeing** on Instagram. I don't post too much, but you can always send me a DM to say hi and or show me pictures of puppies and stuff.

Unicorns are real.

About the Author

Mark Fisher is an international speaker, consultant, and entrepreneur.

Through keynotes, courses, and coaching, Mark helps training gym owners achieve financial success and personal freedom. He's also excellent at playing with puppies, though to date, he has not been paid for this skillset.

Mark and his "non-sexual life partner" Michael Keeler founded Business for Unicorns in 2016 and have since worked with many of the leading fitness studios across the US, the UK, and Australia. Past non-fitness clients include Sony Music, Sylvan Learning, Novus Surgical, and Security Scorecard.

Mark has given keynotes and spoken at events all over the world, including: IDEA World, IDEA Club & Studio Summit, IDEA PTI, Perform Better, FILEX, Anytime Fitness Australia, The Summit by BFS, Lift the Bar, the IFBA, the Fitness Business Summit, the Strong Pro Summit, Vigor Ground Summit, Mike Boyle Strength & Conditioning, Fitness Revolution, and many, many others.

In addition to consulting through BFU, Mark is the co-founder of Mark Fisher Fitness, one of the most unusual gyms in the fitness industry. MFF operates a physical location in midtown Manhattan and an online "virtual" location. MFF was recognized as #312 on the 2015 Inc. 500 fastest growing companies in America, as well as one of Men's Health's "Top 20 Gyms in America."

With a reputation as the fitness home of choice for the Broadway community, Mark and MFF have been featured in Forbes, the NY Times, the NY Post, the Huffington Post, and the Wall St. Journal, among others. MFF has made waves in the fitness industry for its unprecedented success and unique approach to culture. Living their mantra of "Ridiculous Humans, Serious Fitness," MFF provides progressive fitness protocols in a delivery system of subversive humor, fantastical imagery, and outrageous antics. They also inexplicably talk about unicorns, call their clients Ninjas, and treat fun, community, and personal growth as core values.

Mark's newest company, Unicorn Wellness, is an investor in an emerging fitness franchise brand Alloy Personal Training. The first unit is targeting an open date in 2023.

Outside of his fitness business adventures, Mark is a proud alumni speaker of TEDx Broadway, avid Burner, and lover of books, coffee, and cocktails. He currently lives in the Hudson Valley with his wife, Broadway actress Shina Morris-Fisher, their daughter Celestia, and their dog Gizmo.

Like most successful gym owner-consultant-investors, he holds a Bachelor of Fine Arts in Musical Theatre from Syracuse University.

Made in the USA
Middletown, DE
24 October 2023